IS IT WORTH BELIEVING?

THE SPIRITUAL CHALLENGE OF THE

DA VINCI CODE

IS IT WORTH BELIEVING?

THE SPIRITUAL CHALLENGE OF THE

DA VINCI CODE

GREG CLARKE

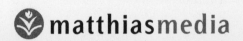

Is it worth believing? The spiritual challenge of The Da Vinci Code
© Matthias Media 2005

Matthias Media
(St Matthias Press Ltd. ACN 067 558 365)
PO Box 225
Kingsford NSW 2032
Australia
Telephone: (02) 9663 1478; international: +61-2-9663-1478
Facsimile: (02) 9663 3265; international: +61-2-9663-3265
Email: info@matthiasmedia.com.au
Internet: www.matthiasmedia.com.au

ISBN 1 921068 17 5

Cover design and typesetting by Lankshear Design Pty Ltd.

Front cover incorporates artwork from the book *The Da Vinci Code*
by Dan Brown, published by Transworld Publishers Ltd, 2003.

CONTENTS

1 | FOR CAVE DWELLERS

*A*FLUSH-FACED STUDENT BARGED into my office at New College and rammed his copy of *The Da Vinci Code* into my hands. "Read this!" he urged. "You'll be out of a job!"

Since there aren't that many openings for people running Christian apologetics centres on university campuses, I took him seriously and read the novel that weekend.

I know I'm in the minority, but it didn't do much for me. To be honest, I thought it was fairly run-of-the-mill murder mystery writing. It had some good pacing, especially early on, but I was put off immediately by the albino assassin. If he hadn't been an albino, I might have been more on board. But the cliché of the albino killer did nothing for my enjoyment of the story. Surely this was just another airport page-turner destined for the bargain bin within a month or two.

But I was intrigued that the novel contained so much religious history. There are pages and pages of 'teaching' from one character to another on the history of Christianity, the early Christian church, how we got the Bible, and discussions of medieval pseudo-Christian sects. Why all of these history lessons padding out a murder mystery?

Meeting with my eager friend the following week, I suggested to him that the novel was built on some well-known speculations about Jesus and the history of Christianity, that it had misused some historical documents that were found in 1945 (*The Nag Hammadi Library*), and that there was no way it would become very popular. No way—it contained too much discussion of ancient religion. And no-one is interested in that!

That was a couple of years ago. I have never been more wrong. The novel has crashed through publishing record after publishing record, spreading wildly across the world of readers, until as I write it is being made into a Ron Howard film starring Tom Hanks. It has topped bestseller lists for longer than most other novels in history.

My friend was wrong, too. My job was not in jeopardy. In fact, thanks to *The Da Vinci Code*, the opportunities to write and speak about ancient Christianity are bigger and better than ever. We Christians have a lot to thank Dan Brown for (NB my tongue is stabbing my cheek).

The Da Vinci Code has put Christian history back squarely on the agenda in popular culture. It isn't alone: Mel Gibson's film, *The Passion of the Christ*, similarly revived public interest in the Gospel accounts of Jesus and no doubt introduced some people to the story of Jesus' crucifixion and resurrection for the very first time. As I write, the film of C.S. Lewis's children's fantasy, *The Lion, the Witch and the Wardrobe* is due for release, with its central story of making 'atonement' for the sins of another (in this case, the lion Aslan dying in the place of the rebellious boy, Edmund). Again, the message of Christianity (that Jesus died for our sins) is up in lights, even if they are sometimes the spotlights of interrogation.

But *The Da Vinci Code* casts its own peculiar shadow over traditional Christianity. Throughout this book, we will explore some of the details of its claims. Since the novel was published, an industry has developed in either defending or attacking its claims. There are already many books that do this well (see the 'Further reading' list at the end of this book). What this book sets out to do is a bit different.

My aim is to examine *why* we come to believe one view of Christianity over another. How do we form those beliefs? What factors contribute to our belief in one thing and our rejection of another? Is it all to do with our family backgrounds or what we were taught at school? Or is it something that we feel deep in our hearts and have little control over? Do reason and logic guide our beliefs, or are we more influenced by what we have experienced or by what the 'authorities' have told us is true?

Is it even possible to change your beliefs, or are you stuck with the ones you happen to find yourself with?

Since this is so important to our assessment of *The Da*

Vinci Code, let's summarize here the various different teachings on Christianity that the characters Leigh Teabing and Robert Langdon proclaim:

- Jesus was not divine. It wasn't until a church council in the fourth century that the Roman Emperor Constantine, motivated by politics, declared that Christians would now believe Jesus to be divine.
- The Bible, in particular the New Testament, was stitched together by another politically driven committee of church figures, once again manipulated into doing it by Constantine.
- There were many alternative accounts of the life of Jesus, which tell a very different story of him than the ones we have preserved as Holy Scripture in the Gospels (those Gospels known to us as 'The Gospel according to Matthew', 'Mark', 'Luke' and 'John'). These alternative accounts were destroyed by Constantine.
- But a few of these alternative 'gospels' survived. Documents found in 1945 in the sands of Egypt tell the true story of Christianity. They are known as *The Nag Hammadi Library*.
- Jesus and Mary Magdalene, one of the women whom the Bible records as followers of Jesus, were in fact married. Mary was carrying Jesus' child, later born in France and called Sarah, when Jesus was crucified (the fact of Jesus' crucifixion is not disputed in *The Da Vinci Code*).

- Jesus did not rise from the grave. There was no resurrection, as Christians believe. There is not a lot of specific discussion of the resurrection in the novel, but the implication is that Jesus died on the cross, and that his line continued through the child Mary Magdalene bore. The story of Jesus' resurrection is derived from the pagan myth of Mithras, the bull-god who was born on December 25 and rose from his tomb after three days—so claim Langdon and Teabing, at least.
- The claims of the Gospels that Jesus did miracles, such as turning water into wine and walking on water, are symbolic, not historical. That is, they provide metaphors and stories which people use to live their lives, but did not really happen.
- Sex is the means by which men and women commune with God. In particular, a man is spiritually incomplete until he has intercourse with a woman. The Church recast sex as sinful and disgusting, in order that it might wrest away for itself the power to act as a conduit to God.

Such material comprises a heavy load for something that fits the unofficial genre of 'airport thriller'!

When you read a novel in an airport lounge, you don't have many study aids around you. You are after diversion and entertainment, not a history or theology lesson. In fact, the point of fiction is to entertain, to pull together facts and fiction into an intriguing story, and to satisfy you by the end, according to the rules of the genre. People differ on whether or not they think Dan Brown has done a good job in the genre, but his efforts have certainly been gargantuan. As we will see, Brown has covered most of the major Christian beliefs, some radical views of sex and human nature, and a vast reworking of the history of groups such as the Knights Templar.

But what happens when you *do* have study aids at hand—when you can check the kinds of claims made by Brown's characters? Does the novel deserve to survive beyond the customs check at airport security? Should it be allowed to influence life in the 'real world'?

In other words, do the views about Christianity that come out of the mouths of the novel's characters provide a fair, truthful, accurate or believable alternative version of Christianity?

Is it worth believing?

Questions like these gave me reason to write this book. But first, we need to introduce the novel.

FOR CAVE DWELLERS

There may be a few of you. People for whom Leonardo Da Vinci is still merely a Renaissance painter, or perhaps a Teenage Mutant Ninja Turtle, and not a member of the secret society that holds the key to a true understanding of spirituality, Christian history and the person of Jesus. There may be a few people who have been living in caves and haven't noticed that a novel called *The Da Vinci Code* has been occupying the minds of train commuters, sunbakers, café diners and distracted university students across the globe.

For the cave dwellers, let me briefly introduce you to this story that has become a worldwide cultural event, and has raised both the fascination and the ire of anyone who has had anything to do with Christianity.

The plot in a page (or two)

Harvard Professor of Religious Symbology, Robert Langdon, is called in by Bezu Faché, captain of the French Police, to investigate a murder. The murdered man is Jacques Sauniére, curator of The Louvre, the famous art gallery in Paris. Langdon's assistance is required, because Sauniére has left a baffling collection of symbolic messages, beginning with the positioning of his own corpse in the shape of Leonardo Da Vinci's drawing, *The Vitruvian Man*. Langdon is joined by Sophie Neveu, an agent of the French Police and a cryptographer—one trained in the science and art of deciphering riddles. Together, they begin to piece together the clues as to why Sauniére was murdered and what secrets he was endeavouring to pass on as he met his demise.

The assassin is, in fact, a tragic figure called Silas, a "hulking albino" who is described as a monk[1] in the Opus Dei group within the Catholic Church. He is doing the dirty work of his Father, Bishop Manuel Aringarosa, who in turn is in the service of a shadowy character called The Teacher

('Aringarosa' in Italian means something like 'red herring'). Together, they have systematically killed off the last remaining keepers of the secrets that Sauniére was attempting to pass on.

These secrets belong to a group called the Priory of Sion, a secret society claimed to have existed since medieval times. Among this group's previous Grand Masters have been famous figures such as Sir Isaac Newtown, Victor Hugo and Leonardo Da Vinci. What secrets does the group hold? Many, but the most startling one concerns the true history of Christianity—that Jesus was not divine, but a mortal prophet who was married to one of his followers, Mary Magdalene.

Clues to this secret history of Christianity can be found throughout the great works of Western art and architecture, for those who have eyes to see them. Robert and Sophie come to realize that the Grand Masters of the Priory of Sion are being murdered to prevent them from making public these secrets of true faith. The Catholic Church, it seems, has a vested interest in maintaining the 'falsehoods' that Christians everywhere believe.

Robert and Sophie learn this alternative history when they visit Sir Leigh Teabing, a wealthy and bombastic scholar who was once Royal Historian and now lives in a castle northwest of Paris. Teabing is fascinated by the legend of the Holy Grail, and has reinterpreted it to refer to this story of Jesus and Mary Magdalene. She is the real Holy Grail, the vessel by which Jesus' influence on the world continues. Teabing is desperate to solve the mystery of the Grail—his

1 | FOR CAVE DWELLERS

life's ambition is to find the final resting place of Mary Magdalene and whatever secrets and treasures might be found with her bones. He will stop at nothing; in fact, he is the Teacher behind the assassinations.

The quest for the Grail accelerates as the different parties race from France to Switzerland to Scotland to England. It ends with the unravelling of Teabing's devious schemes, and the reuniting of Sophie Neveu with her long-lost family—who are, to her great surprise, in the bloodline of Jesus. Finally, Robert Langdon solves the mystery of where the Grail lies—back beneath the Louvre, where the whole adventure began.

Exactly what this all means beyond the pages of the novel remains to be figured out.

What kind of book is this?

In the study of literature, genre is a key to meaning. A book's genre refers to the category into which the book fits—the kind of book it is. Books in a particular genre usually employ similar approaches to the shape of the plot, the style of writing, and the emphasis of the story. And we readers know what to expect from each genre. If the book is a fantasy, we know to expect amazing events that don't correspond to the world of science as we know it. If the book we are reading is a detective novel, we expect a crime to take place, certain clues to be gradually revealed, and the detective to eventually solve the mystery. If the book is a history textbook, we expect it to be communicating as best it can the facts about the past and their significance.

A book can fit into a number of genres and might even twist the rules of the genre for effect, but by and large the genre gives us an indication of what it is that we are reading, what kind of outcomes to expect and how we will get there. It's our major guide to the meaning of what we read.

So what kind of book is *The Da Vinci Code*? What genres does it fit into?

It's a murder mystery, beginning with the assassination of art curator, Jacques Sauniére, and the introduction of the strange, coded messages that this dying man sought to pass on to someone he loved before he breathed his last. It reveals a quest to understand why this man died, who 'dunnit', and what secrets and motives they possessed. We expect there to be suspects. We expect there to be facts and times and dates. We expect there to be red herrings. And we expect a process of reasoning by which we will learn who must be the culprit.

The novel also falls into a category known in literary criticism as the *bildungsroman*, or the 'coming of age' novel. Although it isn't about her childhood, Sophie Neveu comes of age spiritually in *The Da Vinci Code*. It is the story of how she discovers the secrets of her background, and matures in her understanding of spirituality. She learns that her grandfather was a practitioner of an ancient religion—the true form of Christianity—and has to rebuild her views on history, spirituality and sexuality. It might have been titled *The Education of Young Sophie*.

It's also a romance, the story of the unfolding relationship between Harvard Professor and chief investigator (later chief suspect) of Sauniére's death, Robert Langdon, and cryptologist, Sophie Neveu. This is hardly the focus of the book, and indeed it is difficult to believe that much will come of the spark between them (perhaps this is subject matter for the next Dan Brown novel). Nevertheless, the romance genre is important because it relates to what we learn about Jesus and his secret past. It is important that we expect some of the fruits of a romance—there will be attractive characters, 'urst' (Unresolved Sexual Tension) between them, and the slow revealing of the identities of the lovers and why they belong together.

One of the features of romance in *The Da Vinci Code* is disguised identity, a device commonly used in stories from the ancient world to Shakespeare to children's fiction today.[2] Sophie Neveu (the granddaughter of the murdered art curator) discovers by gradual unravelling of the clues left by her grandfather that her true identity is found in the bloodline of Jesus and Mary Magdalene.

And most tellingly, the novel dabbles in historical fiction—a genre that moves between imaginary, made-up worlds, and worlds that we know about from history. It is not itself historical fiction, which would retell events from the past using fictional characters; rather, *The Da Vinci Code* creates an historical fiction within its plot. Through the mouth of Professor Robert Langdon and his historian friend, Sir Leigh Teabing, the reader is led into a world of ancient religion, where history and fiction are blended. The central tenet of the novel is that the history of Jesus and the subsequent history of the church is radically different from what has traditionally been taught. Dan Brown recasts this history of Christianity in a novel way, using the tools of historical fiction to persuade the reader of the veracity of his account.

Don't try to trick us!

Historical fiction is a lot of fun. There's a great deal of pleasure in taking a character who has some presence in the real world (say, a queen or a famous scientist or an explorer) and then imagining that person in novel situations or trying to reconstruct events in full around what we do know in part. Who might have been the seventh wife of King Henry VIII, and what role might she have played in the affairs of sixteenth century England? What did Cleopatra and Caesar talk about as they plotted to rule the classical world? We enjoy this kind of 'factional' storytelling.

But what we deeply resent is when an author works very hard to convince us that what he is writing is fact, when in fact it is fiction.

The human displeasure we experience at being tricked into believing something is real, was brought home to me a few years back when a book of supposed memoirs was published. *Forbidden Love* purported to be the account of Dalia, an Arab muslim woman known to the author, who fell in love with a

Catholic man and was murdered for it at the hands of her own father in an act of 'honour killing'. The author, Norma Khouri, spoke of her book as a tribute to her friend who had died in this way, and an attempt to bring justice and relief to others living under the threat of this practice.

It was a very popular book, moving festival audiences to tears as the author read from it, and prompting politicians to speak out against the honour killings practice. The problem was that it didn't happen. Dalia didn't exist; she hadn't grown up with the author in Jordan; in fact, the author had lived in suburban Chicago with her husband and two kids at the time she was (according to the 'memoir') suffering with Dalia in Jordan.

When it became clear to booksellers that this memoir belonged in the fiction section, some of them made an extraordinary offer—they would refund anyone's money who felt they had bought the book under false pretences.

This incident indicated to me how much as readers we need to trust the author. We care deeply about whether we are being dealt with fairly or being deceived. It really matters to us whether we are reading words that claim to somehow connect with the real past, or words that are about an imagined past. Surely the booksellers could simply have moved *Forbidden Love* from the biography shelves to the fiction shelves—but that would have missed the point. As readers, we really care about whether the author is trying to trick us.[3]

In *The Da Vinci Code*, Dan Brown crosses over that line

of trust. At the beginning of the book, even before the Prologue—in other words, before the fiction begins—we find a page with the capitalized header 'FACT'. On this page, we are given three 'facts', which are to shape the way we interpret the fiction that is about to follow.

Regrettably—outrageously—two of these 'facts' are demonstrably false.

> FACT:
>
> The Priory of Sion—a European secret society founded in 1099—is a real organization. In 1975 Paris's Bibliothèque Nationale discovered parchments known as *Les Dossiers Secrets*, identifying numerous members of the Priory of Sion, including Sir Isaac Newton, Botticelli, Victor Hugo, and Leonardo Da Vinci.
>
> The Vatican prelature known as Opus Dei is a deeply devout Catholic sect that has been the topic of recent controversy due to reports of brain-washing, coercion, and a dangerous practice known as "corporal mortification". Opus Dei has just completed construction of a $47 million National Headquarters at 243 Lexington Avenue in New York City.
>
> All descriptions of artwork, architecture, documents, and secret rituals in this novel are accurate. (*The Da Vinci Code*, p. 1)

We shall discuss the Opus Dei in the next chapter, but of these facts, that's the accurate one. The depiction of Opus Dei practices may be exaggerated, but it is true that they have a large HQ in NYC, and that there are various reports about their particular religious observances and approach to growing their movement that are to some suggestive of a sect. Please withhold judgement on this one until you have read more in the next chapter.

But the other two facts on view here at the beginning of the novel are demonstrably false.

The Priory of Sion is very much the key to the unfolding mystery of the novel. It is the secret society that holds the knowledge of 'true Christianity' that has been hidden from the Church and its adherents for 2000 years. In the novel, a list of supposed Grand Masters of the Priory of Sion is presented, among them Leonardo da Vinci and Isaac Newtown, not to mention the dead art curator and riddle-weaver, Jacques Sauniére.

In a sense, the Priory has a basis in fact, but not in the sense that Brown wants us to believe from his FACT page. The name has a few traceable origins. There are shadowy scraps of information about a monastic order with a similar name, founded in Jerusalem in 1100 and absorbed into the Jesuits in 1617; but I have not been able to find any solid documentation about this. The hard evidence for the Priory of Sion comes into view because of a figure called Pierre Plantard, a French anti-Semite who wished to purify France and believed he had a rightful claim to the French throne.

In 1956, Plantard formed a group called the Priory of Sion with a handful of friends with a similar mindset. This group set about fabricating a set of documents that would prove the existence of a bloodline descending from Jesus and Mary Magdalene, through the kings of France to Plantard himself. Having forged this alternative history, Plantard and his colleagues planted the documents in libraries all over France, including the National Library. He then suggested to some British journalists, Henry Lincoln, Richard Leigh and Michael Baigent, that they look in the Paris Library for new information about the history of Christianity in France. The journos did, and they wrote up the whole imaginary saga in their bestselling book of the early 1980s, *Holy Blood, Holy Grail*. It is this book that provides Dan Brown with much of his material for the stories behind *The Da Vinci Code*.

In 1993, Plantard admitted under oath to a French judge that he had fabricated all the documents relating to the Priory of Sion. The judge warned him not to toy with the judicial system and dismissed him. He died in 2000.

No actual Priory of Sion dating back to the Middle Ages. No list of Grand Masters who knew the secrets about Jesus and Mary Magdalene. No special clues to this spiritual secret in the artwork of Leonardo Da Vinci.

Dan Brown's first 'FACT' is looking more than shaky.

His third fact represents a stunning error in judgement on an author's part. To claim that all of his depictions of artworks, architecture and rituals are accurate is to raise the bar rather high for a page-flipping novel. It places the onus back on him to be able to demonstrate meticulous research and scrupulous presentation of the facts across a very broad range of disciplines. It isn't really any surprise that errors of fact in these areas were found very quickly by readers who do themselves have experience in one or more of these areas. Historians have challenged the history; ritualists have challenged the rituals depicted; artists have questioned the interpretations of art; geographers of Paris have called for the book to be rewritten in the French edition, just to get some of the details correct.

But by making such lofty claims as to the FACTual nature of his writing, Brown sets himself up for a fall. As soon as he is shown to be in error, doubt is cast over the whole project. No longer can we trust the contract between author and reader; he has deceived us before we even reach chapter one. It's not a promising start.

I wonder whether it would cause worldwide economic collapse if booksellers offered refunds for those who come to believe that they have been sold Dan Brown's book under false pretences ...

Evangelistic intentions

On his website, Dan Brown is more up-front about his purposes in writing *The Da Vinci Code*. Although when criticized for errors, he can always remind us that he wrote "a novel", many of his comments reveal an overriding interest in changing the minds of his readers about religion.

He says, "My hope in writing this novel was that the story would serve as a catalyst and a springboard for people to discuss the important topics of faith, religion, and history".[4]

IS IT WORTH BELIEVING?

In fact, in some areas he seems to have a developed agenda for religious reform:

> Two thousand years ago, we lived in a world of Gods and Goddesses. Today, we live in a world solely of Gods. Women in most cultures have been stripped of their spiritual power. The novel touches on questions of how and why this shift occurred … and on what lessons we might learn from it regarding our future.[5]

There is a study guide to the novel that you can download from danbrown.com. It asks not just your usual Book Club questions, but also questions such as "Has this book changed your ideas about faith, religion, or history in any way?" and "Would you rather live in a world without religion or a world without science?" and "For most people, the word 'God' feels holy, while the word 'Goddess' feels mythical. What are your thoughts on this? Do you imagine those perceptions will ever change?"

These are evangelistic questions, questions with a mission to change people's minds and hearts. These come from an author with a mission. And, when faced with people who want to change our hearts and minds, we need to know whether such a change is worth it.

At the end of our introduction, we find ourselves with a romantic murder mystery enfolded in a complicated historical fiction. We know that we want the guy to get the girl, but we are also drawn into believing this alternative history of religion that the key characters explore. This merging of genres puts the reader in a difficult position: it is hard for us to think of this as merely a novel.

Yes, it says it on the cover: "a novel". Yes, it is found in the fiction section of the bookshop. But the nature of the characters' claims, and the way in which the novel is wrapped up in 'facts', suggests that there is some connection between this novel and the world that we, the readers, live in.

This is a novel that is meant to change our lives. Its claims are so extraordinary, and if true outside of the novel would have such enormous implications for Christianity as it is currently practised—not to mention how the history of religion would need to be rewritten—that this novel deserves prolonged attention of the critical kind.

And it has been getting it.

ENDNOTES

1 There are, in fact, no monks in the Opus Dei association. Only official religious 'orders', such as the Jesuits or the Benedictines, have monks. Opus Dei is an association of laypersons and priests founded in 1928. This small error is one of many that add up to shake our confidence in the novel's claims to be historically accurate. For the association's own response to *The Da Vinci Code*, see Opus Dei, *The Da Vinci Code, the Catholic Church and Opus Dei*, Information Office of Opus Dei on the internet, 2005, viewed 23 August 2005, <http://www.opusdei.org/art.php?w=32&p=7017>.

2 E.g. Harry Potter's discovery that, contrary to his lowly position in the care of the Dursleys, he is in fact a wizard.

3 For the investigation of Khouri's claims, see Malcolm Knox, 'How a 'forbidden' memoir twisted the truth', *The Age*, 24 July 2004, viewed 23

August 2005, <http://www.theage.com.au/articles/2004/07/23/1090464860184.html?oneclick=true>.

4 Dan Brown, *The Da Vinci Code: Common Questions*, Dan Brown, viewed 23 August 2005, <http://www.danbrown.com/novels/davinci_code/faqs.html>.

5 Dan Brown, *The Da Vinci Code: Common Questions*.

2 | CRITICISMS AND APOLOGIES

$\mathcal{I}$N ONE SENSE IT is obvious how *The Da Vinci Code* has been received.

With open wallets.

At the time of writing, there are nearly 25 million copies in print in 44 languages. The book rocketed to the top of the charts, and stayed there for years. According to *Publishers Weekly* (the prayer book of the publishing industry), the book debuted at the top of the list and stayed there for 120 weeks.[1]

People have plainly enjoyed this novel, and it has created an excessive cultural phenomenon. Now you can take *Da Vinci Code* tours in Paris and in Edinburgh and investigate the artwork and architecture mentioned in the novel. The Rosslyn Chapel in Scotland (scene of the novel's *denouement*) has reported a 56% increase in visitors since the release of the novel.[2] Dan Brown must take a great deal of credit for this—he wrote a book that hooks people in and takes them on just the kind of ride they like.

Those in the business of reviewing books have both praise and ridicule for *The Da Vinci Code*. New York Times critic, Janet Maslin, called the novel, "Blockbuster perfection. An exhilaratingly brainy thriller." "Not since the advent of Harry Potter", wrote Maslin, "has an author so flagrantly delighted in leading readers on a breathless chase and coaxing them through hoops".[3] But some reviewers have been critical to the point of cruelty, feeling that the author's lack of expertise in many of the areas he covers demands a belittling response. One Chicago art historian wrote, "[T]here seems to be an opera lurking in these pages, and Mr Brown could do worse than weigh the immortal advice of Voltaire: 'If it's too silly to be said, it can always be sung.'"[4]

Despite these voices of protest, a vast number of people have found the book riveting, 'un-put-downable' and in some way liberating. It has done for many adults what the Harry Potter books have done for adolescents—got them reading again. 25 million of them.

Sales figures alone clearly don't explain the novel's popularity. There have been other murder mystery/romances that deserved the same attention from a large public. There have been better written, better plotted and more exciting airport thrillers. Why has this one stood out so prominently?

The more cynical among us might suggest that it is the victory of marketing. With the rise of the internet, email and other forms of instant communication, people can spread the word very quickly about a new 'sensation'. Still, what made the noise about this book rise above the already high decibel level of advertising that we all experience? [5]

We might ask whether the book is popular simply because it is controversial. It certainly has a plethora of 'targets'. And targeted, unhappy people do a lot for a book's sales. Among the book's targets are Catholic Christians (in particular a group called Opus Dei), scholars of the history of Christianity, art historians (especially those up to speed on Leonardo da Vinci), Parisians, Londoners, theologians, Scots, scholars of the form of religion known as Gnosticism, medievalists, mathematicians, Walt Disney, and fans of the movie, *The Lion King*!

Having included in his story speculations and claims that, if true, would undermine the beliefs of all of these people, Dan Brown was well-positioned to make an impact when he published.

THE RELIGIOUS REACTION

And make an impact he did. Within months of the appearance of the book, and its spectacular ascent to the top of the sales charts, the 'targets' began firing back. A quick visit to Amazon.com reveals over two dozen religious critiques of the novel, many of them suggesting their approach in the titles: *Cracking the Da Vinci Code, Breaking the Da Vinci Code, The Da Vinci Hoax, The Da Vinci Deception.*

The attacks made by the characters of the novel on traditional Christianity are deep and at the root. It is no surprise that people who believe the traditional view took exception to the novel and came out against it.

A number of authors of these books were interviewed and asked why they felt the need to write detailed, often aggressive, polemics against a novel which might just as easily be ignored as airport entertainment. I found their reasons for writing intriguing. Here's a selection of their responses.

Amy Wellborn, author of *Decoding Da Vinci* (Our Sunday Visitor, Inc., 2004):
It was obvious that some readers were not, indeed, looking at this book as 'only a novel'. Their faith was disturbed, their assumptions undercut. It was clear to the publisher and me that these questions deserved answers. Hence the book.

Darrell L. Bock, professor of New Testament studies and author of *Breaking the Da Vinci Code* (Nelson Books, 2004):
The key was when I heard Dan Brown on national TV say that if he were writing nonfiction he would not change a thing about the history. Not only that, but he said he had heavily researched his work and had become a believer in these views. It was then I decided that this was not just a novel, but was being portrayed to the public as something more.

James L. Garlow, Californian pastor and author of *Cracking the Da Vinci Code* **(Cook Communications, 2004):**
When I first heard about the book and its claims, I didn't take it seriously. In fact, I told people that it was just fiction and everybody would surely regard it that way. But I was wrong. People started believing it.

Ben Witherington III, professor of New Testament studies and author of *The Gospel Code* **(Intervarsity Press, 2004):**
These indeed seem to be ... times when people will believe things that are 'beyond belief'. This book is intended as a wake-up call to those who have not been noticing the signs of the times.

There are some common threads among the reasons given for writing. Certainly, all the Christian critiques wish to register their objection to the Dan Brown version of Christianity. No surprises there. As we have already seen, Brown's novel offers an entirely revised version of the faith that millions of people around the world hold as true.

But a second aspect of the motivation for writing stands out—concern for the beliefs of Dan Brown's readers. All of these authors feel a strong and compassionate desire to warn people about being misled. They don't want to see people believing the unbelievable just because it came to them in the form of a gripping mystery novel.

Sure, it is possible that all of these Christian writers are part of the bigger conspiracy to keep the 'real Christianity' away from people, to maintain the status quo and conserve the church's power over people's lives. But their quotes just don't sound as paranoid as that. They really do seem concerned that readers don't take on board what to these Christian writers deserves to remain squarely on the shelves marked 'fiction'.

As one further example of a religious response to the novel, let's look at the Opus Dei section of the Catholic Church. This group really is painted in grim colours in *The Da Vinci Code*. The novel's assassin, the albino Silas, is described as a monk belonging to this 'order'. His father in the faith, Bishop Aringarosa, is "president-general" of the Opus Dei and resides in a palatial residence in the movement's headquarters in New York City. Aringarosa is a man driven by ambition for the Church and for the Holy Grail. Through their tanglings with 'The Teacher', Silas and the Bishop pursue a bloody path of holy killings, only to end up destroying each other in the process.

After he has committed the murders as requested, Silas does penance by flagellating himself and wearing around his thigh a spiked cilice, a leather belt with sharp metal spikes on it. Through this suffering, he is supposed to purge himself of the guilt for the murders he has committed in his Church's name.

The Bishop and Silas learn that the Vatican intends to revoke its sanction of the Opus Dei—to boot their group out of the Catholic Church. Throughout the novel, Dan Brown emphasizes the controversial practices (alleged) of this group: corporal mortification, aggressive recruitment of vulnerable people by doping them, oppressive attitudes towards women. Towards the end of the novel, Opus Dei is described as "a liability and an embarrassment" (*The Da Vinci Code*, p. 544/416).[6]

What does the Opus Dei make of its depiction in *The Da Vinci Code*? After all, the novel blends certain facts about the movement (its headquarters in NYC, its foundations in the book *The Way* written by conservative Spanish priest, Josemaría Escrivá) with error (it is not a monastic order, but the opposite—a lay organization).

The Opus Dei has sought to respond to the novel with information. On their website (www.opusdei.org), they have a series of articles exploring and explaining their teaching on physical suffering, on the allegations of cult behaviour, on wealth and power, and on the place of women in the Church. Their claim is that Dan Brown has caricatured them and exaggerated their practices for the sake of his novel. Their hope is that people will step back from the novel and consider the Church that they find in the real world, if they do a bit of investigating. For instance, the novel claims that the Opus Dei attitude to women is archaic and oppressive, forcing them to be "acoustically and visually separated" from men in their buildings (*The Da Vinci Code*, p. 49/28). In response, the Opus Dei website offers a quote from the founder of Opus Dei, St. Josemaría Escrivá, concerning the status of women:

I see no reason why one should make any distinction or discrimination with respect to women, when speaking of the laity and its apostolic task, its rights and duties. All the baptized, men and women alike, share equally in the dignity, freedom and responsibility of the children of God ... For many reasons, including some derived from positive law, I consider that the distinction between men and women with respect to the juridical capacity for receiving Holy Orders should be retained. But in all other spheres I think the Church should recognize fully in her legislation, internal life and apostolic action exactly the same rights and duties for women as for men.[7]

With this information, the reader is then in a position to ask him or herself this question: OK, I have the story of the novel and the information from the organization that exists in the real world. Now, who will I believe, and why?

I am not here either to defend or condemn the Opus Dei. What I wish to point out is that there are ways of working out whether or not to believe the stories told about the Church in the novel. There is real-world information to be gleaned; real world bishops to listen to; and real world religious practices to observe. As readers, we have to use all of these resources to work out whether or not what we have read in *The Da Vinci Code* is worth believing.

Eventually, the Roman Catholic Church has come to take this novel very seriously. A senior Cardinal, Tarcisio Bertone, the Archbishop of Genoa, has become an anti-*Da Vinci Code* spokesman, urging people not to buy the book nor read it and describing its religious claims as "shameful and unfounded".[8] He has expressed frustration that many people will have their first exposure to Christianity via this novel, and has set about to run seminars and lectures to counter this state of affairs.

In summary, Christian people have reacted in three ways to *The Da Vinci Code*.

1. They have objected to it. Catholics and Protestants have opposed the presentations of religion that are made in the novel. They have pointed out errors of fact, errors of exaggeration, and errors of cultural misunderstanding.

2. They have expressed deep concern for other readers, not in a condescending manner but with real interest in the way people will come to their decisions about Christianity. There is an anxiety that we may have a generation of people who have been informed about Jesus only through this novel.

3. They have attempted to offer an 'alternative to the alternative'. Churches have invited people to read the biblical Gospels in order to see the portrait of Jesus, Mary Magdalene and the disciples that is painted there. They have recognized that it is not enough to object to a version of Christianity; it is also important to offer an alternative message that connects with people's needs.

MY REACTION

Having explored some of the reactions from Christian people to the novel, permit me some navel-gazing. What about me? How did I find it? I've mentioned my reactions in the first chapter (and I feel I took a risk there of alienating anyone who has just loved the book, but if you are still reading, I take it I wasn't too harsh).

In order to flesh out my response, I need to provide some biographical background.

I was raised by two Christian parents, and I can't recall a time when I didn't know the account of Jesus as given to us in the Bible. I resented this a little as a teenager, wishing I had a better 'testimony', with an amazing conversion account possibly involving a wild storm, a near-death encounter and a flashing moment of spiritual insight. But that was not to be!

My mum and dad taught me from the Bible, took me to Sunday School and youth clubs. I imbibed the story of Jesus as the Lord of the universe, the one who came from God the Father into the world in flesh on that first Christmas 2000 years back, spoke the wisest of words, gave miraculous signs to indicate who he was, and then died in a manner that satisfied God's anger at sin. He was then raised back to life by God, victorious over death and sin and giving us hope of an eternity with him. This understanding of who Jesus was came to shape my place in the world and my understanding of how life should be lived.

So how would someone like me, a standard Christian,

respond to a novel that was saying that everything I have believed is wrong?

I surprised myself with what happened as I read the novel. A word kept coming into my head:

SORRY

As I read, I felt a genuine need to say sorry to others who were reading the novel. As Leigh Teabing and Robert Langdon began to offer up their own interpretations of Christian history, I started to understand what they were getting at. Their attacks on Christianity began to hit their target. It wasn't that I felt guilty of all the accusations made, nor did I feel that their descriptions of the Church's actions always reflected the kinds of churches I've been involved in; nevertheless, I felt this need to say sorry for at least three things.

Sorry ... that the Church has sometimes hidden the truth from people.

My first instinct was to apologise for the failures and blindness of the Church. By 'the Church', I mean any large group that is claiming to worship Jesus Christ as the Son of God, Lord and Saviour of the world. What I am about to say probably applies equally to other large institutions such as governments and corporations (maybe even families), but I have in mind here religious groups that can be summarized as 'the Church'.

It is true that the Church has sometimes hidden the truth from people. Here is the view of Sir Leigh Teabing, when he is explaining to Robert Langdon how the Catholic Church is murdering members of the Priory of Sion in order to suppress the Magdalene story. Langdon wonders why knowing the 'truth' would rattle the Church. Teabing replies:

> "What about those who look at the cruelty in the world and say, where is God today? Those who look at Church scandals and ask, who *are* these men who claim to speak the truth about Christ and yet lie to cover up the sexual abuse of children by their own priests?" (*The Da Vinci Code*, p. 356/266)

This is one of the until-recently unspeakable facts about the Church. She has, indeed, covered up immorality within her ranks. One of the great steps forward of our time has been to pull back the covers on such horrors as child sexual abuse by priests, and start down the long road to making amends where possible for this stupendous betrayal of trust.

And if the Church can hide such heinous sins within its ranks, what else is it capable of hiding? It suddenly becomes clear why people would be attracted to the idea that the church was hiding a secret as big as the identity of Jesus and Mary Magdalene. When trust has been betrayed, then anything seems possible.

Furthermore, the Church becomes a bully in people's eyes. When there are secrets to be kept, people have to be stood over in order that they don't let the secrets slip out.

"My dear," says Teabing to Sophie Neveu, "the Church has two thousand years of experience pressuring those who threaten to unveil its lies" (*The Da Vinci Code*, pp. 533-4/407).

Many people perceive the Church as an irresponsible bully, flushed with power but having lost perspective on the heart of morality. She has become blind to the wickedness that she is perpetuating. Corruption enters the ranks of those in charge, and they will do anything to keep their hold on power.

Of course, not everyone's experience of the Church is like this—not even most people's. And by no means are all priests and church leaders guilty of sin and corruption to this extent. Nevertheless, it seems appropriate to apologise for the wrongs that have been done and recognize that *The Da Vinci Code* taps into the very common feeling among the 'post-Christians' of today's world that the Church can't be trusted.

Sorry ... that the Church can seem like a 'masculine'-only place, where women are second-rate citizens, ignored or oppressed.

It is also true that, in the opinion of many, the Church is a place where men are in charge and women are secondary. *The Da Vinci Code* taps into the oft-expressed opinion that the Church (like many institutions and societies) is a patriarchy, and a domineering one at that. This novel expresses the frustration of many people with the place of women in society and the Church. Although, as I shall explain, I believe the direction that the novel charts for a feminisation of religion is wrong-headed and misunderstands what Christianity teaches about men and women, nevertheless I felt a strong sense of sadness that so many women would feel this way about the Church.

I felt sad that one of the reasons the novel is so popular is that it acknowledges this and offers an alternative. And I felt a real need to apologise to women who feel this way about the Church. Surely, God does not want any woman to feel denigrated, oppressed, ignored or second-rate. And I know many women do (not to mention some men).

Even women who have never set foot in a Church can be of the view that the Church is somewhere women aren't welcome—at least not in a 'seen and heard' manner.

So what kind of feminine religion does *The Da Vinci Code* offer?

Unfortunately, it offers one that moves so far away from a biblical understanding of gender and relationships that it really isn't the answer to the Church's dilemma over women. It is tied, instead, to the legend of the Holy Grail.

Robert Langdon offers Sophie an understanding of this teaching, which we will need to explore in some detail:

"The Grail is literally the ancient symbol for womanhood, and the *Holy* Grail represents the sacred feminine and the goddess, which of course has now been lost, virtually eliminated by the Church. The power of the female and her ability to produce life was once very sacred, but it posed a threat to the rise of the predominantly male Church, and so the sacred feminine was demonised and called unclean. It was *man*, not God, who created the concept of 'original sin', whereby Eve tasted of the apple and caused the downfall of the human race. Woman, once the sacred giver of life, was now the enemy [...]

"The Grail", Langdon said, "is symbolic of the lost goddess. When Christianity came along, the old pagan religions did not die easily. Legends of chivalric quests for the lost Grail were in fact stories of forbidden quests to find the lost sacred feminine. Knights who claimed to be 'searching for the chalice' were speaking in code as a way to protect themselves from a Church that had subjugated women, banished the Goddess, burned nonbelievers, and forbidden the pagan reverence for the sacred feminine." (*The Da Vinci Code*, pp. 321-2/238-9)

This complex version of femininity is, as Langdon admits, drawn from pagan not Christian sources. Teabing and Langdon claim that Christianity corrupted this earlier, better understanding of womanhood in order to instate male power in the new religious order of the Christian Church. According to Langdon, only when the feminine is restored to the central place in spiritual understanding will human beings again grasp their place in the cosmos.

At this point, the novel's big mystery can be unwrapped. *The Da Vinci Code* is a quest for the Holy Grail. In traditional understanding, the Holy Grail is the vessel from which Christ drank at the last meal (the famous 'Last Supper') he spent with his followers (disciples) before he was arrested and sentenced to death by crucifixion. In

Catholic teaching, it is also the vessel used by Joseph of Arimathea to catch the dripping blood of Christ as he hung on the cross. Legend has it that Joseph travelled to Britain in AD 63 with the sacred cup but it was lost, hence the many quests to find it by King Arthur's Knights of the Round Table and others.

The startling claim of *The Da Vinci Code* is that the Holy Grail is not a vessel at all. It is a person—in fact, it is a particular person, a follower of Jesus called Mary Magdalene, who was married to Jesus. Specifically, Mary's womb is the Grail. It is the vessel that carried the blood of Jesus, as it conceives the child who will continue this Holy Family's line in the world.

We will examine the evidence for such a claim later, but for now the important point to make is that part of the appeal of this claim in the novel is that it stands against many people's (especially) women's experience of Church. It places femininity at the heart of religion. We are given a clue to the importance of this idea in the name of Sophie Neveu. 'Sophie' (or 'Sophia') means 'wisdom' in Greek, and 'Neveu' means 'new' or 'grandchild' in French. We have, embodied in the person who carries this name, the new spiritual wisdom—the woman who is in the bloodline of Jesus, the intelligent, delightful, courageous, riddle-cracking daughter of the last Grandmaster of the Priory of Sion.

Before leaving this apology to sink in, there are a few points to be made in Christianity's defence.

- Jesus loved women. Although it is going too far to say,

as Leigh Teabing does, that "Jesus was the original feminist" (*The Da Vinci Code*, p. 334/248), he certainly treated women in a manner superior to the prevailing culture. At least three women travelled with him (see the Gospel of Luke 8:1-3). He accepted attentions from women in a way that was startling to the men around him (see Luke 7:36-50 and John 12:1-8). Furthermore, the biblical Gospels are very unusual for their time because they record the witness of these female followers of Jesus to his resurrection from the dead; traditionally, female witness would not be considered acceptable.[9]

- Let's admit it, the Bible doesn't sit squarely with many current cultural views on gender. There are difficult passages in the Bible (difficult to our contemporary ears, that is) that can be stumbling blocks for many people who might otherwise be interested in finding out about Jesus. For instance, the teaching in Ephesians 5:21-33, about what it means for husbands to love their wives and wives to submit to their husbands, often jars when 21st-century people who haven't grown up on the Bible hear it in a wedding service. It isn't easy to explain in a few sentences how Christians put together these passages of Scripture into a coherent understanding of male-female relations, but I do want to acknowledge that many Christians sit strangely to our culture at this point. We look weird.

- The traditional Church often struggles to explain its thinking on this topic. We don't have a great track record of entering into dialogue and discussion about why we do things that seem out of sync with the culture around us. Usually, the reason is that we think the Bible is teaching us something different, and it trumps the views of the culture of our day. It's not all our fault: the media rarely gives us a fair opportunity to explain what we mean.

- These issues of gender can be a stumbling block to taking seriously the other aspects of the message of Jesus Christ. My hope is that they will not be insurmountable, and that perhaps aspects of the Christian message can be considered before the issue of gender gets on the agenda.

It needs to be said that this novel's attacks on the Church's attitude towards women are not all fair. The Church is not guilty of all the charges made against her in this novel. The documents of both the Catholic and Protestant churches are not misogynistic in the way the novel claims. However, there is still room for a very significant apology for when Christian people have not lived out true Christianity in the way they have treated women.

Sorry for the abuse. Sorry for ignoring women. Sorry for inappropriately silencing them. Sorry for not giving their contribution the value and the high praise that it deserves.

This theme of an alternative feminine spirituality is surely one reason this novel is so popular.

Sorry ... for not presenting the truth as we understand it in an exciting, attractive and believable way.

One final apology kept coming to mind as I was reading *The Da Vinci Code*.

Sorry for being boring.

Christians have sometimes made the reality of Jesus about as appealing as diced liver (more apologies, this time to offal fans). Christians can make Christianity seem mundane, restrictive, all about rules, or all about denying yourself pleasures. If we do, we are presenting a distorted view of Christianity.

If you think that Christianity is about rules, restrictions and denials, I can understand why *The Da Vinci Code* is such an attractive alternative:

- It makes you excited about spirituality again
- It makes history come alive
- It helps you think about the mysteries of life
- It presents a very human portrait of Jesus and Mary
- It debunks 'hard' traditional beliefs and gives you alternative forms of history, sexuality and theology.

The Da Vinci Code offers a view of religion that can seem more human, more in contact with the real world, more about relationships and experiences and love and sex and celebration. In contrast, Christianity might be summarized as an old building, an old book and old bodies in pews.

But genuine Christian beliefs are far from dull. Our claims for Jesus alone are nothing short of astounding. We think he is the key to understanding the purpose of life. We think he opens up the opportunity of freedom, hope and mercy for all people who believe in him. And we believe that he rose from the grave and in doing so demonstrated his power over the things that we fear most. We're excited by these spiritual ideas. But I fear that because of the failures of the Church, the tension over the place of women, and our laziness in presenting what we see as the exciting truth, we still have a lot of work to do to earn a hearing.

I have offered some critiques of the novel's claims in this chapter, but I have equally wanted to offer my apologies. Christians are definitely guilty of some of the claims of this novel, and I for one am sorry about it.

ENDNOTES

1 Publishers Weekly, Reed Business Information, New York, 22 August 2005, viewed 23 August 2005, <http://www.publishersweekly.com>.
2 'A chapel's link to the Holy Grail', *Sydney Morning Herald*, News, 24-25 July 2004, p. 8.
3 Reproduced at Dan Brown, *The Da Vinci Code: Reviews*, Dan Brown, viewed 23 August 2005, <http://www.danbrown.com/novels/davinci_code/reviews.html>.
4 Bruce Boucher, *Does 'The Da Vinci Code' crack Leonardo?'*, The New Age Center, 2003, viewed 23 August 2005, <http://www.newagepointofinfinity.com/new_page_10.htm>.
5 There may be a 'secret' explanation for why the book became so popular, along these lines. Apparently, the publisher sent out a whopping 10,000 advance copies of the novel to publishers, editors

and reviewers, including some very significant website reviewers.
One of them, Francis McInerney, was a Top Ten reviewer at
Amazon.com at the time of the novel's release, and is thanked in
person in the Acknowledgements at the beginning of the novel.
No news spreads faster than news on the web! See Nick Paumgarten,
No. 1 Fan Dept. Acknowledged, The New Yorker, 28 April 2003, viewed
23 August 2005, <http://www.newyorker.com/talk/content/?030505ta_
talk_paumgarten>.

6 Page references are first to the UK/Australian edition of *The Da Vinci
Code*, published by Bantam Press, and then after the forward-slash to the
US hardback edition, published by Doubleday.

7 From an interview published in *Palabra*, October 1967 (Spain), and
republished in *Conversations with Josemaría Escrivá*, Scepter Publishers,
New York, 2002. Reproduced at Opus Dei, *Opus Dei and women*,
Information Office of Opus Dei on the internet, 2005, viewed 23
August 2005, <http://www.opusdei.org/art.php?w=32&p=9313>.

8 Richard Owen, 'Vatican plots against "Da Vinci Code"', *Times Online*,
15 March 2005, viewed 23 August 2005, <http://www.timesonline.co.uk/
article/0,,11069-1525702,00.html>.

9 New Testament historian Darrell L. Bock notes that this last fact
adds weight to the historical truthfulness of the Gospels in the Bible:
"This detail, running against the larger, ancient culture as it does, is
one of the key evidences that these resurrection stories were not
invented by a church trying to give Jesus a higher status than he really
had. Had believers merely invented these appearance-and-tomb stories
with the hope that they would convince the culture about Jesus, they
would not have unanimously picked women to bear the story's burden
to be true." Bock, *Breaking the Da Vinci Code: answering the questions
everybody's asking*, Nelson Books, Nashville, 2004, pp. 138-9.

3 | THE DAN BROWN SCHOOL OF KNOWLEDGE

$\mathcal{W}$E COME NOW TO the reason I wanted to add another *Da Vinci* book to the growing pile. Dan Brown's novel has performed for us what we might call 'The House Fire Miracle'. I happen to know a number of people whose houses have burned down entirely. Living in a weatherboard house with a wife who loves candles, I sense that it is merely a matter of time before we join them.

The house fire provides a severe mercy (less severe if your insurance is up-to-date). Your whole life's structure goes up in flames. All of the possessions you hold dear are suddenly unreachable, blackened beyond recognition, never to return. You realize that some of them didn't actually matter as much as you thought they did. You grieve and ache over the ones that still did. But you also don't have to think about the small details that have cost you sleep for months—whether the kitchen cupboards need replacing, or how to get the coffee stain off the TV room wall.

Suddenly, you are starting again, able to reset your priorities, your use of time, what you will buy, and what you won't bother with. The deadwood of your life has gone and you see yourself in a new, scarily focused way. You feel your burdens have been lifted.

You know what is worthwhile, and what is not.

PERHAPS THIS IS YOU. Perhaps you went through a kind of 'burning down the house' experience when you were reading *The Da Vinci Code*. Ideas about religion that you had previously assumed were the case—that the Bible told us the truth about Jesus, or that Jesus rose from the dead on Easter Sunday—might now have been challenged, or even tossed aside with the excitement of new discoveries.

Perhaps the novel confirmed some suspicions for you: you had always wondered whether Jesus was really divine, or whether the Church had made this up. Or maybe you had thought that the Bible was put together by human hands and the novel has now given you further reason to believe that.

If this is you, then you may already have moved from one set of beliefs to another. You may have moved on from your initial beliefs about Christianity into something new—a Sophie Neveu-style 'new wisdom'.

Or you are at least wondering whether you should.

This book is first and foremost meant for you. It is trying to address that question: "Is it time to move on from those old traditional beliefs? Is there something better to believe?"

As may already be obvious, my view is that the answer to that question is no. *The Da Vinci Code* presents an alternative to the traditional, long-held understanding of Christianity, but it is not a view that is worthy of your belief. I have been introducing some of the reasons why the novel falls short of the qualities required to be believable, and we still have more to consider. But in this chapter, we first think about *why* the views in *The Da Vinci Code* have been attractive to many readers, possibly you. What explanations are there for its success? What explains the attraction of the ideas about religion that Leigh Teabing and Robert Langdon proclaim with such confidence?

THE SPIRIT OF OUR TIMES

One explanation for why *The Da Vinci Code* has been so popular is that it taps into the spirit of our times. We have already explored this a little in the previous chapter. The novel focuses on the way people feel about the Church— about institutional authority. We hate the fact that the Church acts hypocritically, hiding immorality in its ranks while it preaches goodness and virtue. The novel also makes a good deal of the rise of feminism and gender issues in Western society. Its account of the 'sacred feminine' is not (in my view) a very coherent one, but it is nevertheless built on the general mood of our times that male dominance and patriarchal society structures have caused a great deal of harm and need to be reconsidered.

These are just two of the 'flashpoint' issues in today's Western societies, which we have already touched on. One other very important flashpoint that the novel visits is the question of knowledge. *The Da Vinci Code* challenges preconceived ideas of how we gain knowledge—especially religious knowledge and historical knowledge. In other words, the novel raises for discussion the question of how we come to understand the past and how we come to understand the spiritual side of life.

On these questions, *The Da Vinci Code* has an 'in vogue' approach. You can almost hear the remembered phrases of first year arts and humanities classes in the dialogue Dan Brown uses for his characters. "What is history, but a fable agreed upon?" says Leigh Teabing, quoting Napoleon. "By its very nature, history is always a one-sided account" (*The Da Vinci Code*, p. 343/256). "Every religion describes God through metaphor, allegory, and exaggeration", Robert Langdon instructs Sophie Neveu (*The Da Vinci Code*, p. 451/341). These are views that have been made popular in university arts faculties over the last 50 years.

With due respect to the effort Dan Brown has put into

researching *The Da Vinci Code*, we can't expect to find coherent philosophical reflection within it. It is not the kind of book that will help you put together a comprehensive understanding of history or religion. We only receive snippets of café-variety philosophy and history here and there out of characters' mouths as they are used by Dan Brown to expand the plot and put together the various elements of his mystery thriller. It would be wrong to lean on a few aphorisms from Leigh Teabing for your take on God. Wouldn't it?

But I am getting ahead of myself.

What are these contemporary views of knowledge that the novel expresses? I want to consider at least six.

1. We are suspicious of people trying to sell us something or wield power over us. We particularly don't like authority figures.

Technically, this is called a 'hermeneutic of suspicion'.[1] In ordinary words, it means that whenever someone is telling us 'the truth', they are also trying to wield a certain amount of power over us. If someone knocks on the door of your house around about dinner time, they are usually trying to sell you a cheap phone service. They will show you documents revealing that their service is cheaper than their competitors, and that they can give you the best possible deal. They will present statistics, offer promises and make up slogans (e.g. "The best deal on the block") to persuade you that what they are saying is true. But we all know that what they in fact want is to lock us into a contract that means we will stick with their phone service for a good length of time and they won't have to knock on our door again.

It is possible that these salespeople are telling the truth and presenting us with accurate information, but if you are anything like me, your immediate response is one of suspicion. "They don't really care about giving me the best phone deal", I will be muttering to myself. "What they want is control of my phone. It's not about the knowledge, it's about power." At which point, I politely decline the offer.

We are deeply suspicious today (often rightly so) that when people claim to have the truth and want to tell it to you, more is going on than simply communication. Claiming to have the truth gives the claimant a degree of power and influence over those who don't have it. Their 'texts' can be a cover-up, or a device, in order to gain that power.

The flipside is that those who believe such claimants (for example, church-goers who believe what priests tell them, or patients who believe their doctors) are sometimes viewed as 'sheep'—people who don't really know what they believe and why, but have just followed along with what an authority figure told them.

The intellectuals who explored this idea in most detail were the German philosopher, Friedrich Nietzsche, the French theorist, Michel Foucault, the psychologist, Sigmund Freud and the political philosopher, Karl Marx. Each of these thinkers became 'suspicious' that claims of truth within their disciplines were actually masking grabs for power.

Marx analysed religion and saw in it not issues such as salvation and the afterlife, but a way of dulling people's sense of life's mystery in order to make life bearable. He famously said that religion was like opium for the people—rather than being the knowledge of reality, it is a drug that helps us escape reality.

Nietzsche thought that religion was used to enslave people by turning weaknesses into strengths; he thought that concepts such as pity and compassion were actually misguided ways of protecting those who had no hope and were better off dead!

And for Freud, religion was a kind of illusion that satisfies our inner drives for a father figure and a sense of belonging. Believing a religion to be true is really, according to Freud, just a way that we fulfil our longings. It doesn't connect with reality.

Foucault, the most radical of all these philosophers, takes the idea one step further and says that we can never really know the motivations behind our claims to 'know the truth'. We are always just pretending to understand why we believe things to be true. It is really just a strange outcome of the way we play games with language. We say something is true, but we never really know what we mean by that. However, what we do see happening is that people with power define what is considered true by others.

You may be hearing in your mind echoes in *The Da Vinci*

Code of the ideas of these 'masters of suspicion'. They are ideas that have come to be commonly held in our time—perhaps they are similar to your own views. Perhaps you are convinced that religion is an illusion, perhaps a 'crutch', as it is often called. Perhaps you can see that people use claims of religious truth to achieve their political purposes, or to keep someone in their place ("Don't do that, or God will punish you!").

Certainly, this is the view that Leigh Teabing expresses in the novel concerning how we got the Bible and why Christians believe that Jesus is divine.

Teabing tells Sophie Neveu that "the fundamental irony of Christianity" is that "[t]he Bible, as we know it today, was collated by the pagan Roman emperor Constantine the Great" (*The Da Vinci Code*, p. 313/231). He then relates his own version of how we came to have the Bible. Teabing's claim is that Constantine cleverly manipulated his subjects (including a large number of powerful bishops and church figures) to create the kind of Christianity that he thought would further the empire.

> "Constantine commissioned and financed a new Bible, which omitted those gospels that spoke of Christ's *human* traits and embellished those gospels that made Him godlike. The earlier gospels were outlawed, gathered up, and burned [...]
>
> "[T]he modern Bible was compiled and edited by men who possessed a political agenda—to promote the divinity of the man Jesus Christ and use His influence to solidify their own power base." (*The Da Vinci Code*, p. 317/234)

We will need to unpack this quote. Leigh Teabing puts forward as fact a number of theories about the origins of the Bible. He suggests that there were thousands of different accounts of who Jesus was, written by his many followers, and that in the majority of these documents Jesus is described as a mortal man—a great man, but not divine. These gospels have by and large been lost, the novel claims, and the reason is that Constantine rounded them up and destroyed them. Constantine wielded his power to manufacture 'the truth' that Jesus is divine.

Furthermore, Teabing claims that Constantine used his weight as emperor to sway the view of a major church council (known as the Council of Nicea, which gave the world the Nicene Creed) to assert that Jesus was divine when in fact they knew he was just a man.

"My dear," Teabing declared, "until *that* moment in history, Jesus was viewed by His followers as a mortal prophet … a great and powerful man, but a *man* nonetheless. A mortal."

"Not the Son of God?"

"Right", Teabing said. "Jesus' establishment as 'the Son of God' was officially proposed and voted on by the Council of Nicaea."

"Hold on. You're saying Jesus' divinity was the result of a *vote*?"

"A relatively close vote at that", Teabing added [...]

"It was all about power", Teabing continued. "Christ as Messiah was critical to the functioning of Church and state. Many scholars claim that the early Church literally *stole* Jesus from His original followers, hijacking His human message, shrouding it in an impenetrable cloak of divinity, and using it to expand their own power. I've written several books on the topic." (*The Da Vinci Code*, pp. 315-6/233)

Notice how much these quotes are in keeping with the spirit of our times—we expect authority figures to control what we call 'the truth' in this way.

But Teabing's view in the novel does not correspond with anything we know of history in the real world. We will leave the details of this until the next chapter, except to put on record, as an indicator of just how wrong Teabing can be, that the 'vote' by the 300 participants at the Council of Nicea recognizing (as opposed to 'proposing') Jesus' divinity was not exactly close: it was 298-2!

2. We feel that *no-one* has special access to 'The Truth'.

This is perhaps the most potent effect of the era of ideas that we live in, which is often described as 'postmodernity'. In the postmodern era, the idea that some people have the Real Understanding of life, while others are entirely wrong in their beliefs, is not at all popular. Although people can still be quite elitist and snobbish about how right their views are compared to others, most people believe the snobbery is unfounded—the poor snobs are deluding themselves.

Philosophers call this an "incredulity towards metanar-ratives",[2] which means that people these days find it hard to accept that there is a big, overarching explanation of what life is about (a 'metanarrative', a big Truth). Again, a certain suspicion is evident in us.

This position might be construed as a very humble one. After all, there is a kind of egalitarianism about no-one having the ultimate answers. But let's not be overly generous at this point. The usual form that this incredulity takes is to point out how foolish someone else is for in fact holding to a metanarrative.

Dan Brown expresses this view succinctly in an interview on his website. He says:

> The world is a big place and, now more than ever, there is enormous danger in believing we are infallible; that our version of the truth is absolute; that everyone who does not think like we do is wrong, and therefore an enemy [...]
>
> [O]ur male dominated philosophies of absolutism have a long history of violence and bloodshed which continues to this day [...]
>
> My critics and I clearly have read different books and have had different teachers. Some of these people sound absolutely certain of their truth, and of that I am envious. As I said, I was not born with the luxury of absolute certainty.[3]

The mood of our times includes a degree of antagonism towards anyone who claims to be certain about what they believe. In fact, Leigh Teabing and Robert Langdon demonstrate their urbane intellectualism by revealing just how wrong religious adherents are.

But this is not the whole picture on our contemporary

attitude towards religious knowledge. As *The Da Vinci Code* demonstrates, there is an abiding fascination with the notion that there is secret truth, that some people have found it and others haven't, and that we might be able to go on quests, decipher codes or receive secret messages in order to gain a glimpse of it. Dan Brown confesses to still being on the quest to discover the secret:

> I really wish I had the luxury of absolute unquestioning faith. I do not, and I am still searching. I wrote this novel as part of my own spiritual quest. I never imagined a novel could become so controversial.[4]

Despite the egalitarian outcomes of the loss of absolute certainty, many of us are still eager to be the ones with true spiritual insight. There is still something elitist about *The Da Vinci Code* and its claims that only a handful of Priory of Sion Grand Masters really understood the true history of Jesus and the true nature of the Holy Grail.

We may not believe in metanarratives, but we still like to have secret knowledge and we still search for it. We are such inconsistent creatures!

3. We feel that everyone has access to some kind of truth.

To offset our inconsistency concerning spiritual insight, we do like to think that everyone has at least some grasp of the truth. This is called pluralism, and it is a widespread belief today. Again, looked at kindly it springs from a sort of humility and generosity, a desire that everyone be considered worthy of truth. It is a feature of our common humanity that all of us would be correct about at least some of life. Surely no-one has entirely fallacious beliefs.

This approach to knowledge leads us to notice the similarities between religions rather than the differences. It also requires some challenging mental games of *Twister*, as we seek to reconcile vastly different notions of God, reality, humanity and the purpose of life. The broad approach we take in order to ensure that everyone has at least part of the truth is to remove the specific claims of a religion or worldview and replace them with generic terms. Thus, the death of Jesus on a cross as the means of forgiving sin becomes but one expression of the generic good work of sacrificing yourself for the people you love. Or the message of the Bible that there will be a day when God will judge the world for its deeds becomes the generic idea that we have to take responsibility for our actions.

In this way, those of us swept up in the postmodern approach to knowledge can accommodate a vast range of religions, ideologies and worldviews.

Sophie Neveu's grandmother, Marie Chauvel, makes just this move near the end of the novel. Having spent the entire novel on a quest for the Holy Grail, identified as Mary Magdalene and the sacred feminine, Robert Langdon's perspective is challenged by Chauvel. She turns the quest for Mary Magdalene, the womb of Christ's bloodline, into a generic spiritual quest.

"It is the mystery and wonderment that serve our souls, not the Grail itself. The beauty of the Grail lies in her ethereal nature [...] For some, the Grail is a chalice that will bring them everlasting life. For others, it is the quest for lost documents and secret history. And for most, I suspect the Holy Grail is simply a grand idea ... a glorious unattainable treasure that somehow, even in today's world of chaos, inspires us." (*The Da Vinci Code*, p. 581/444)

Funnily enough, this reinstates the concept of a grand metanarrative. But it gives us a metanarrative without any *specific* story line. It is like one of those books you can have made for your children where the plot is there in outline, but you ask the bookshop to overprint your children's names, the names of their pets, their favourite activities, and the ending that you think will leave them most satisfied.

In order to think everyone has access to the truth, we have to relax the technicalities of what that truth entails. It is based on the view that genuine spiritual knowledge is not specific; the specifics are just accidents of your birth and your culture. You are a Muslim because of where you were born and who raised you; likewise, an atheist, a Christian or an apatheist.[5] The specific beliefs don't really matter.

4. Consequently, we find it hard to accept that some people may have true beliefs and others might not.

This is the outcome of what can be called a pragmatic approach to knowledge. It makes it nearly impossible to challenge another person's beliefs. Not only is it seen as a move to enforce your own metanarrative on the other person, but it would also suggest that there is Truth out there somewhere such that one person's own beliefs might not be sufficient to understand life and live it well.

There are some healthy ethical sentiments in this position. No-one enjoys being told they are wrong, or even suggesting that one set of beliefs might fit with experience better than another. And because many people have suffered insults and inconvenience at the hands of over-zealous religious types, knocking on your door and thrusting salvation into your hands like a time-bomb, they are rightly wary of getting into the business of critiquing other people's beliefs.

That's fine, but if we surrender our faculties of criticism entirely, we end up in a very strange position with regards to knowledge. We end up saying that no knowledge is in fact solid or trustworthy, but that we shouldn't worry about that because it might upset people. This amounts to intellectual suicide.

Robert Langdon has a rambling conversation with Sophie Neveu late in the novel which comes around to precisely this point:

> "The Bible represents a fundamental guidepost for millions of people on the planet, in much the same way the Koran, Torah, and Pali Canon offer guidance to people of other religions. If you and I could dig up documentation that contradicted the holy stories of Islamic belief, Judaic belief, Buddhist belief, pagan belief, should we do that? Should we wave a flag and tell the Buddhists that we have

proof the Buddha did not come from a lotus blossom? Or that Jesus was not born of a *literal* virgin birth? Those who truly understand their faiths understand the stories are metaphorical." (*The Da Vinci Code*, pp. 451-2/342)

While I can sympathize with Langdon's compassionate motives for suggesting that we should never disenchant someone whose beliefs can in fact be shown to be false or contradictory, I also feel that he is being condescending here. He is taking the position of Jack Nicholson's character in the movie, *A Few Good Men*: they can't handle the truth!

We need to reflect on what a serious and disturbing position has been taken. Langdon is suggesting that, although the beliefs of religious people might be shown not to match with reality as we know it now (Langdon seems to mean scientific reality in the quote), we should not dispel these myths because they are doing a good job of providing meaning for people's lives. Fake meaning, but meaning nonetheless!

Sophie Neveu responded to Langdon's wisdom with scepticism:

"My friends who are devout Christians definitely believe that Christ *literally* walked on water, *literally* turned water into wine, and was born of a *literal* virgin birth."

"My point exactly", Langdon said. "Religious allegory has become a part of the fabric of reality. And living in that reality helps millions of people cope and be better people."

"But it appears their reality is false."

Langdon chuckled. "No more false than that of a mathematical cryptographer who believes in the imaginary number 'i' because it helps her break codes." (*The Da Vinci Code*, p. 452/342)

Langdon thus parallels religious beliefs with mathematics—they are merely intellectual tools to get the job of living done in a satisfying manner. This pragmatic approach to knowledge reflects a deep suspicion that we cannot really connect the world of our ideas, thoughts and beliefs with the 'real world'. We can only come up with concepts that seem to satisfy our intellectual, emotional and spiritual needs. But there is no guarantee that they match anything beyond our own experience.[6]

I know mathematicians who would want to defend the reality of numbers, but that aside, can this view of knowledge really be the case? Surely there are religious beliefs, which, if true, have real-world consequences (likewise if false). For example, if a Christian believes that by doing miracles such as turning water into wine, Jesus gave those around him a glimpse of his divine calling, then it matters whether the miracles in fact occurred. If Jesus turned water into wine in the first century, without the aid of a laboratory, then it does tell us something about his power and authority. If he didn't, then he is either a liar or just a mortal (as Teabing believes), or both.

Conversely, if people hold beliefs that can be shown to be false, fabricated or contradictory, then it is in fact a compassionate thing to point this out. This is particularly true if the beliefs have consequences. You might be very sensitive about the time and place at which you point out the problems, but to leave people in ignorance is hardly benign when their ignorance may lead to their harm.

Because of the specific teachings of Christianity, we Christians find it impossible to accept the pragmatic view of knowledge. We cannot go along with the 'as long as everyone feels good about it' approach to truth. If Christianity is in fact true, it teaches that there is a God who will call the world to account for its deeds, its words and even its secrets. If that is in fact true, it would be cruel and neglectful not to make people aware of how we can be saved from God's judgement on that day of account.

While at first glance the mood of our times seems tolerant and compassionate—'let people hold their beliefs, since it helps them get on in life'—it is in reality a careless and hard-hearted approach to take to other people. If a person's beliefs have important consequences (and many do), it is far more loving and generous to explore whether the belief is worth holding. We will do some assessment of the worthiness of beliefs in the next chapter.

5. We have an 'add rather than divide' approach to religious knowledge.

The character of pluralism is to be eclectic, to gather beliefs and ideas and customs like a magpie. Instead of discerning between beliefs, a pluralist adds more beliefs to his stable. He often does not pause to consider whether those beliefs can happily exist side by side without brawling. He sees the connections between things rather than the obstacles that divide them. We are told that Robert Langdon has this view of knowledge early in the novel: "[…] Langdon viewed the world as a web of profoundly intertwined histories and events. *The connections may be invisible*, he often preached to his symbology classes at Harvard, *but they are always there, buried just beneath the surface*" (*The Da Vinci Code*, p. 32/15-16).

At times, it seems that the pluralist view of knowledge challenges the law of non-contradiction. In the study of logic, the law of non-contradiction states that something cannot be P and not-P at the same time. For example, the statements "I am a son" and "I am not a son" cannot both be true. That may sound obvious, but it is amazing how often people can try to slip around this basic law of thought, subconsciously or consciously.

I once took a Bible class in which there was a lovely woman called Jane who was about to teach Scripture lessons in her children's school. She had grown up a Catholic, but had not spent much time herself reading the Bible. Now that she had been asked to teach others, she thought it was time to find out what she was going to teach them!

We read part of the Letter to the Romans together, from the New Testament, and as we read Jane's eyes took on a startled look. She seemed to be shocked by what she was reading. "This isn't the St Paul I knew!" she said, shaking her head. I guess she had been given some other version of St Paul from the pulpit.

As a group, we talked about Paul's explanation of how a

person does not receive salvation by their good deeds, but by Jesus Christ's sacrifice for sins when he was crucified. Throughout the discussion, Jane looked quite shaken.

"But we are saved by our good deeds! That's what I have always believed."

I replied that the Bible was telling us that we are not—we are saved by Jesus' good deed of sacrifice, on our behalf.

At this point, Jane paused. She thought hard, and seemed to be coming to some sort of decision. After a few seconds, her brow suddenly relaxed and she began to smile.

"That's it", she said. "They are both right. My priest and St Paul are both right."

"But the Bible says we are *not* saved by our good deeds, Jane!" It was my turn to feel agitated.

"Yes, but my priest and St Paul are just approaching the issue from different angles", she replied. "It's okay. I'm happy with that now."

That happened some 10 years ago and it still troubles me. Jane was in effect saying that the statements "We are saved by our good deeds" and "We are not saved by our good deeds" are both true. Somehow, in her own mind, she had reconciled these two propositions in a way that made her feel happy to believe both of them. Perhaps she had developed some theological subtlety that enabled them to fit together, but I doubt it. Rather, she had simply become another pluralist when it comes to knowledge. She was adding rather than dividing.

Please don't hear me to be saying that all religious beliefs are black and white. Far from it. There is plenty that it is difficult to understand and where being 'dogmatic' is probably inappropriate. But my objection is to the idea that we can simply add beliefs together, without any concern for whether they contradict each other or cancel each other out.

The Da Vinci Code takes the 'adding' approach. The Rosslyn Chapel, where Sophie Neveu is reunited with her grandmother and brother, and where Robert Langdon solves the mystery of Saunière's poem about 'Roslin', is a monument to pluralism. Dan Brown writes:

> [...] the chapel is engraved with a mind-boggling array of symbols from the Jewish, Christian, Egyptian, Masonic and pagan traditions [...] Every surface in the chapel had been carved with symbols—Christian cruciforms, Jewish stars, Masonic seals, Templar crosses, cornucopias, pyramids, astrological signs, plants, vegetables, pentacles, and roses [...] Rosslyn Chapel was a shrine to all faiths ... to all traditions ... and, above all, to nature and the goddess.
> (*The Da Vinci Code*, pp. 564, 567/432, 434)

This chapel is a concrete expression of the idea that all religions, cultures and beliefs might somehow fit together, sitting side by side in a grand and complex expression of either the oneness of faith, or the fact that all believers are just as deluded as each other (the novel has a bet both ways). This kind of pluralistic knowledge really is difficult to sustain once we move beyond the mere displaying of different religious symbols side by side on the walls of a chapel. The religions and philosophies mentioned in the quote above contain many points of direct contradiction. For example, Christians believe that Jesus is God's promised Messiah; Jews believe that he is not. Christians believe there is a heaven; Ancient pagans believe there is not a heaven.

These are major differences. In our endeavours to be inclusive and honouring to believers of all kinds, we need to keep before us the realities of religious beliefs. They do not all fit together without serious breaches of the law of non-contradiction. Religious pluralism just does not add up.

6. We believe in a kind of spirituality but not in dogma.

The final idea we will consider concerning how we approach religious knowledge these days is dogma. 'Dogma' has become something of a swear word; to call someone 'dogmatic' is rarely a compliment. It suggests someone who is rigid, not open to nuances and shades of grey, bloody-minded about their own scheme of things and unlikely to change their mind for anyone.

While I do know people who fit this description, dogma gets some undeserved bad press. It means something like 'principles laid down by an authority'. We have already discussed the difficulties our contemporary culture has with authority. We also have difficulty with 'principles'. We are very uncomfortable with the suggestion that an idea (say 'stealing is evil') is so obviously and universally true that we can call it a principle of human morality.

"But it all depends on the situation", we might object. "Perhaps he had starving children to feed."

"It was just a small adjustment of his expenses for taxation purposes", another complains.

"I was just downloading the song to try it out and forgot to delete it afterwards", says someone else.

We can always think of reasons why a belief shouldn't be 'set in stone', but should be more fluid and changeable.

In some areas of life, this is certainly the case. Not all virtuous human behaviour can be clarified in a principle that lasts throughout ages and cultures. Sometimes, flexibility and adaptability are essential to living a moral life. However, the tendency of our times is to move pretty much *all* kinds of knowledge into this flexible condition.

But there is some knowledge that you need pure and simple, in principle form. For instance, it is a principle (dogma) of the Christian faith that God created the universe. We can argue about how he did it, what he created, and whether it involved a Big Bang, but it is nevertheless a basic Christian teaching that God did it.

This idea of simple enduring principles seems to be very unpopular today. *The Da Vinci Code* builds on the sense many people have that the dogma of the Church does not relate well to truly spiritual living. A good spiritual life seems to many of us to require great flexibility of beliefs rather than faith in certain enduring principles. Dogma has been replaced with the more encompassing and harder-to-define notion of spirituality.

In his book, *Stirrings of the Soul*, Australian missionary and theologian Michael Raiter, writes:

Once spirituality is cut loose from any confessional basis then the truth of an experience becomes self-validating. One can discover one's own private and personal spirituality. The issue is not so much one of truth or virtue, but it is simply utilitarian; it works for you. I have no right to judge what works for you. My only obligation is to respect the diversity of beliefs and experiences and to affirm you in what gets you through the night.[7]

Where dogma and religious doctrine are seen to be dry, life-less and disconnected from our lives, spirituality embraces our lives and makes them richer. Marie Chauvel speaks of "the mystery and wonderment that serve our souls" (*The Da Vinci Code*, p. 581/444), symbols and emotional experiences and exciting ideas which all lift the spirit without being tied down to any specific teachings about who God is.

There is, of course, a great deal that is good about this kind of spirituality. Wonder, deep feeling and rich experience of life are not to be frowned upon. But they shouldn't come at the price of ignorance. In *The Da Vinci Code*, we are offered a kind of spirituality that may seem attractive, but it comes at the cost of disregarding what has actually happened in history. Langdon and Teabing's version of Christianity comes at a high price—the distortion of history and the speculative intermingling of mythology, symbolism and theology in a way that disregards even the basic rules of good scholarship. Again, the details will come out further in the next chapter.

Christians may have to shoulder some of the blame for the move away from Christian principles/beliefs and towards a more vague spirituality. We have probably made Christian dogma seem overly obscure and complicated, full of arcane debates on God's Trinitarian being and what it means to be justified, sanctified and glorified. These complex theological points are sometimes important, but even when they are, they make Christianity seem remote and obsessed with the minute details of beliefs—in other words, dogmatic.

It isn't supposed to be like that. Jesus explained who God was to the ordinary people of the first century Middle East. His followers were fishermen and shopkeepers, not divinity professors (to be honest, there were a couple of those, too). The poet Dryden got it right:

> Faith is not built on disquisitions vain;
> The things we must believe are few and plain.[8]

Christianity, even when it is dogmatic, is meant to be attractively plain and simple to grasp.

With that admission of guilt in place, our society does need to reflect on whether we pay too high a price for the kind of spirituality that we like and crave. It may be that such spirituality is a bit like partying on a sinking ship, oblivious to the reality of the iceberg that is right in front of your path. Although it may enrich our lives in the short term, the question must be asked whether it has enough to offer the needy human soul over the long term.

AFTER THE FIRE

If reading *The Da Vinci Code* caused a House Fire Miracle for you, tossing your notions of religion into the air so you could watch them come down in flaming embers, please stop to consider why. It may be that the explanation is found in some of these contemporary approaches to knowledge and belief that we have been considering.

Are you suspicious of authority, dismissive of the idea of capital-t Truth, with a tendency to add beliefs to each other rather than compare and contrast them, and a liking for non-dogmatic spirituality?

If so, you are no doubt among many companions, since these are the attitude towards knowledge and belief that are most common in the early twenty-first century Western world. They are the seedbed into which the religious claims of *The Da Vinci Code* are planted.

As I have tried to make clear, there is at least something commendable in this attitude towards knowledge—it's not all being rubbished here. But there is also a great deal that needs to be questioned, and in my view will be found wanting. In this chapter, I have outlined some of my contentions with postmodern and pragmatic views of knowledge. In the next chapter, I want to take the self-examination a step further to ask what criteria we use for assessing the beliefs we have.

ENDNOTES

1 The phrase "hermeneutics of suspicion" was coined by recently deceased French philosopher, Paul Ricoeur. It refers to a method of interpretation that assumes that the literal meaning of a text is often a mask for the political goals the text is serving.

2 This phrase was introduced by Jean-Francois Lyotard in a book called *The Postmodern Condition* in 1979.

3 To listen to the talk, go to <www.danbrown.com/media/audio/ DVC_NH_talk.mp3>. For a useful discussion of this talk, see Tom Price, *Dan Brown: Looking behind the code*, Damaris Trust, viewed 23 August 2005, <http://www.damaris.org/content/content.php?type= 5&id=388>.

4 <www.danbrown.com/media/audio/DVC_NH_talk.mp3>.

5 A fabulous word for a person who really doesn't care whether or not there is a god. There's even a website: <www.apatheism.net>.

6 For those interested in philosophy, an American called Richard Rorty currently champions this school of pragmatism. Rorty's influence on popular culture is on the rise; I have no idea whether Dan Brown is a Rorty fan, but the ideas expressed by Langdon here are pure Rorty. See Rorty's home page <http://www.stanford.edu/~rrorty> and for a Christian critique of his views, see Dean Geuras, *Richard Rorty and the Postmodern Rejection of Absolute Truth*, Leadership University, 13 July 2002, viewed 23 August 2005, <http://www.leaderu.com/aip/docs/ geuras.html>.

7 Michael Raiter, *Stirrings of the Soul: Evangelicals and the New Spirituality*, Matthias Media, Sydney, 2003, pp. 91-2.

8 John Dryden, 'Religio Laici' ('A Layman's Faith'), 1682.

4 | I BELIEVE BECAUSE ...

*W*HAT EXACTLY ARE BELIEFS? A fair definition might be: "Propositions held to be true." That is, a belief is something you could put into a sentence (e.g. "Cats are the best pets") and ask someone whether he or she thinks your sentence is true. The answer would tell you what that person believes. You might ask the person to "Prove it!" (especially if you happen to be a dog lover), but even if they couldn't present you with any evidence as to why cats are the best pets, this wouldn't prevent them from holding the belief. They might even say to you, if you bothered them for long enough, something like "I don't need any evidence; I just know its true", or "Only an idiot would think cats weren't the best pets", or "My family has always been on the cats' side".

When they do this, they are providing you with an *expla-*

nation for their belief. They are letting you in on some information about why they have the belief.

Philosophers argue about whether we choose beliefs, or whether we just have them. At present, the majority is of the view that we just have them, that we find ourselves believing something and can't be quite sure how we came to that point. Beliefs seem to come to us spontaneously and without our control. When someone asks you how you came to believe something, it can be quite hard to answer him. Try it out on some friends: ask them how they came to believe that it is good to be happy. It's very hard to respond!

The famous Oxford professor and novelist, C. S. Lewis, author of *The Lion, the Witch and the Wardrobe* tells the story of his conversion to Christianity in a way which helps to understand this.

After a long period of time discussing myths, the New Testament, points of theology, and the figure of Jesus with friends and colleagues such as J. R. R. Tolkien (author of *The Lord of the Rings*), Lewis came to believe that there was a God. He used to call himself an atheist, but through these discussions, through logical argument and through his own reading and thinking, he came to the view that there is some kind of god. However, it was more than a year later before he became a Christian, and when he attempts to describe the method by which he came to believe Christianity to be true, he cannot:

> I know very well when, but hardly how, the final step was taken. I was driven to Whipsnade one sunny morning.

When we set out I did not believe that Jesus Christ is the Son of God, and when we reached the zoo I did [...] It was more like when a man, after long sleep, still lying motionless in bed, becomes aware that he is now awake.[1]

Lewis was a deep reader and thinker—he had invested a great deal of time and effort exploring the beliefs that he didn't hold. But then he suddenly found that he held them!

I suspect this is entirely normal. We just have beliefs—we suddenly find that they are in our minds. But we are also aware that our beliefs can be *changed*, be it for good reasons, bad reasons, no reason, or just about any reason. We can't force ourselves to believe things, but we certainly change our minds about things when other ideas come along that appeal to us. And one of the amazing skills that human beings have is the ability to ask ourselves questions: "Why do we believe that? Is it a good idea to believe that? Should we continue to believe that?" We can interrogate our own beliefs.

The most disciplined of us can be very reasonable, weighing up evidence, reading books, thinking about arguments and exploring the consequences of beliefs (as did Lewis). As a reader of this book, I'm guessing you would fall into that category. But many people have their beliefs for fairly slight reasons—dad told them, they saw it on TV, or it 'feels right'. Yet more people cannot really explain why they have certain beliefs; and yet, have them they do, often adamantly.

In this chapter, we will look at the explanations for our beliefs: why we hold them. I have been emphasizing through this book that we need to ask ourselves whether it is *worth believing* the claims that are made about religion in *The Da Vinci Code*. As we look at the various explanations we have for our beliefs, we will consider more of the details of *The Da Vinci Code*'s claims about Christianity. And we will ask whether those claims amount to anything worth believing.

Each of the explanations given below can be either a good one or a bad one for holding a particular belief. We will think about which it might be when it comes to believing *The Da Vinci Code*.

I BELIEVE BECAUSE ... IT'S WHAT I GREW UP WITH

The Swiss psychologist Jean Piaget studied the way children's minds develop from birth until after puberty. He found that children go through stages of development to progressively become more capable of abstract thought. While we become aware of ourselves at around age two, it is not until we are nearing 12 that we have much capacity to think about abstract ideas such as ethics, justice and whether something is worth believing.

These limits to our development mean that we have done a lot of living before we are able to reflect on the kinds of information that has been 'downloaded' into our brains by our parents, our teachers, the books we have read, the television we have watched and the experiences that we have had.

So there is little point feeling any resentment for finding yourself in your late teens with a set of beliefs and not really knowing how they came to be yours. Welcome to the human experience!

But at that point in late adolescence, we are able to ask the question, "Why do I believe these things, and am I going to keep believing them?"

The temptation of many teenagers is immediately to answer, "No way!" It's time to rebel from parents and set your own path in a different direction—*away* from those old pelicans with their fuddy-duddy ideas.

But that can hardly be the obvious answer. After all, what if you have been given extremely reliable and valuable instruction as a young child, such that the beliefs you hold match with reality very well? You would be insane to give them up simply for a chance at rebellion.

There must be more to sorting out what is worth believing than simply rebelling against your parents.

A different approach is to ask yourself this: when you look at other people who have grown up with similar beliefs, do their beliefs seem justified? This can give you some perspective on your own situation. If you have a friend who grew up in a similar culture, with similar religious teachings and similar life experience, take a look at what he or she believes. Do the beliefs seem reasonable? What would you want them to reconsider or cast aside?

It seems to me that *The Da Vinci Code* takes the 'rebel against your parents' line, but with a twist. In this case, the 'parents' are the official Church and its teachings about Jesus and the religious life. These must be rejected in order to reach spiritual maturity. The novel falls into the genre of *bildungsroman* (coming of age) novels, as was mentioned earlier in this book, since its aim is the education of Sophie Neveu about true Christianity, about her own place in the bloodline of Jesus, about the sacred feminine, and about a new form of sexuality. She has to rebel against the orthodox understanding that is prevalent, and take on the new beliefs.

But should she?

I BELIEVE BECAUSE ... IT LOOKS AND SOUNDS RIGHT

One of the explanations we often give for our beliefs is that they 'seem right'. We have a complicated sense inside us—a blend of our emotions, our thoughts and our perceptions— that just brings us to believe something. It is sometimes called intuition; at other times, 'the ring of truth'. In the Australian movie, *The Castle*, a shambolic lawyer named Dennis Denuto has to appear before a magistrate to defend a case against the eviction of the lovable Kerrigan family from their 'castle'. When asked to explain why he believes the eviction is unfair, the lawyer responds: "It's just the vibe, your Honour."

We believe plenty of things just because of 'the vibe'.

And it's not always a bad measure. Human beings have an in-built sense that certain things are right and wrong, fair and unfair, and we can usually get a great deal of agreement between people about these things. For instance, most people feel bad about lying—they think it's wrong.

The flipside to believing something because it feels right is *not* believing it because it feels wrong. This, too, has some value, as we are often able to detect in a general, maybe subconscious, way that something does *not* have the ring of truth about it or is counter-intuitive.

But our intuitions about right and wrong are certainly not failsafe. They are easily corrupted.

Take politicians. They seem to begin their careers with a degree of idealism, promises to be honest and not to mislead the electorate, and attempts to deal with everyone fairly and equally. But the pressures of office seem to mount very quickly, and before long they are re-interpreting their initial promises as "not really appropriate now given the change in circumstances" and doing favours for people who can keep them in power. Where a politician might stand vehemently for an issue one day, he or she 'flip-flops' the next. Eventually, politics starts to look like a conscience-free zone—not helped by the fact that only occasionally do political parties allow a 'conscience vote' on an issue!

But before we point the finger at others, we know ourselves how conveniently we change our position according to the benefits of the situation. Nevertheless, we also still feel the twinges of conscience when we act against our 'inner voice'—against the vibe.

Although our intuitions may be a good general guide—a rule of thumb—we can't depend on them alone to make judgements. The 'vibe' can be ignored, distorted or dulled beyond influence. Hence the need for laws and courts and appeals and all of the legal rigmarole that entails our justice system.

A number of appeals to intuition are made in *The Da Vinci Code*. These are claims that something is worth believing because it seems to be true, it feels right or it matches with our intuitions. The first is the idea that Jesus was married. As we know, the novel suggests that Jesus was married to Mary Magdalene and that the Church has suppressed this fact because it somehow detracts from Jesus' divinity. Evidence is brought forward for this view, as we shall see, but the appeal is also made to Sophie (and us) by Leigh Teabing that it really just makes sense that Jesus was married:

> "As I said earlier, the marriage of Jesus and Mary Magdalene is part of the historical record [...] Moreover, Jesus as a married man makes infinitely more sense than our standard biblical view of Jesus as a bachelor." (*The Da Vinci Code*, p. 330/245)

When Sophie asks why, Teabing's reply is in two parts: one, Jewish custom of the time forbade men to be celibate (an appeal to the evidence of history); two, "[i]f Jesus were not married, at least one of the Bible's gospels would have mentioned it and offered some explanation for His unnatural state of bachelorhood" (*The Da Vinci Code*, p. 330/245). This second part is an appeal to our intuition—we just feel that the Bible should have explained why Jesus was single and celibate.

So does this approach make it reasonable to believe that Jesus was married?

I don't think so, also for two reasons. The first is that Teabing's intuitions on this issue spring from inaccurate information about Jewish customs. He refers to Jesus as a 'rabbi' and, since rabbis customarily did marry, Jesus must have, too. But Jesus *wasn't* a rabbi, even though some people called him that. He had no official religious position. So there is no reason for him to have followed that custom.

Secondly, it doesn't say anywhere in the Bible, or anywhere in ancient literature, that Jesus was married, but there is discussion to suggest he was single. In Matthew 19:12, Jesus himself refers to the fact that some people remain single for the sake of the kingdom of heaven. Quite clearly, it wasn't so unusual to be a bachelor.

Another area in which the novel challenges us to believe because it 'sounds right' is the history of the Priory of Sion. Throughout the novel, we are provided with an elaborate and fascinating account of this secret society, allegedly one of the oldest such societies on earth (*The Da Vinci Code*, p. 158/113). We are told that Leonardo da Vinci presided over the group in the early sixteenth century, and other luminary figures were also Grand Masters—Sir Isaac Newtown, Victor Hugo, all the way down the years to Sophie Neveu's grandfather, Jacques Saunière. It is slowly revealed to us that this society held the secret knowledge of the meaning of the Holy Grail, the story of Jesus' marriage to Mary Magdalene and his desire that his church continue through her bloodline. As the novel's plot unfolds, as we begin to understand, along with the characters, that the Catholic Church is hunting down Priory members before they let leak this new religion that would pull the rug of authority from under the Vatican's feet.

Within the structure of the novel, the history of the Priory works as a remarkably clever device for a murder mystery. It provides the secret identities for key characters such as Saunière (the Grand Master), Teabing (the Teacher) and Sophie (the unsuspecting Royal Princess); it helps explain the actions of villains; and it provides the clues needed for the cross-continental quest for the location of the Holy Grail.

But is there anything that is worth believing about the Priory of Sion when we close the novel's final page?

At this point, many readers have responded with something like this: "Yes! The Priory sounds plausible to me. We know the Church tries to hide secrets from people, and we have a feeling that Jesus might have been married. We can easily believe in a secret society from the Middle Ages that knew things about Jesus that have since been suppressed. Yes! It feels believable. What's more, there are all sorts of documents recording its history—aren't there?"

Some amusing mock press releases have been floating around the web, suggesting that the President of the United States has spoken out against the Priory, and that military action against the Priory "could not be ruled out at this point"![2]

This sense that something like the existence of the Priory could be the case—let's call it the conspiracy vibe— fits rather well with our culture's expectation that there is someone, somewhere, behind the scenes pulling the strings. But in this case, it is based on very little other than the vibe itself. As we explored earlier in this book, the Priory of Sion seems to be a religious and historical hoax conceived by Pierre Plantard in 1956 in France. Shadowy references to a small order of monks in the 12th century have no bearing on this allegedly all-powerful secret society that has kept the truth of Jesus under wraps for centuries.

Our willingness to accept as believable something from fiction, itself drawn from a hoax, says a great deal about our imaginations. We are very influenced by exciting alternatives to what we see on the surface of life. We have intuitions that tell us that powerful institutions *do* get involved in cover-ups and people *do* work behind-the-scenes of contemporary life. We are willing to accept the possibility of something like the Priory, and sometimes this possibility turns into a genuine belief.

But, in this case, we need to challenge that belief because of the demonstrably false information on which it is based. In this case, our sense that 'it feels right' needs to be labeled an 'Aringarosa'—a 'red herring'.

One more intuition that needs to be resisted is the sense that Leonardo Da Vinci knew the 'secret' of Jesus and Mary Magdalene's marriage.

The suggestion of the novel is that Leonardo hid within his paintings clues for the wise as to the true history of Jesus. The most telling instance of this is his depiction of one of the disciples in his famous mural, painted on an enormous wall of a convent in Milan, known as *The Last Supper*. According to traditional interpretation of Renaissance painting, the figure sitting to the left of Jesus from the viewer's perspective is John, the disciple whom Jesus loved, as the biblical Gospel of John describes him in at least five places (e.g. John 13:23). However, Leigh Teabing instructs Sophie Neveu that the figure is actually a woman—"flowing red hair, delicate folded hands, and the hint of a bosom" (*The Da Vinci Code*, p. 327/243)—and a particular woman, Mary Magdalene, Jesus' wife. Furthermore, the shape of the mirror-image bodies of Jesus and 'Mary' in the painting makes a phantasmal letter 'M'. A quick glance at the painting suggests that this is all true—yes, the figure looks feminine, and yes, there appears to be an 'M'.

So, if the claims of Leigh Teabing about this painting *look and feel* right, are we justified in believing it to be true?

Only if other information doesn't come along to show that it is unlikely.

In this case, such information does come along. To begin, the figure of John is the standard type in Renaissance painting for a protégé—fine-featured and clean-shaven. Furthermore, the condition of the painting is very poor, and has been since just a few decades after it was painted (thanks to Leonardo's choice of materials). According to one Leonardo scholar, "There is not enough of any of the faces left to make any serious determinations".[3] And finally, the 'M' seen in the painting most likely has more to do with Leonardo's use of triangles and pyramids in artistic composition than it does with religious symbolism.

Anyway, even if it could be proven that Leonardo had intended to paint an image of Mary Magdalene in his *Last Supper*—so what? Would this tell us anything at all about whether Jesus and Mary Magdalene were married? Why should we think that a fifteenth century artist had the information about Jesus that no-one else had? Why would we believe him rather than the documents of ancient history?

Sophie Neveu understands this: "I'll admit, the hidden M's are intriguing," she says to Teabing, "although I assume nobody is claiming they are proof of Jesus' marriage to Magdalene" (*The Da Vinci Code*, p. 330/245). Teabing agrees, and adds that "the marriage of Jesus and Mary Magdalene is part of the historical record". This introduces new criteria for belief: evidence. We shall think about that shortly.

In summary, we all have instincts about what is true that

can be relied on—sometimes. And we have a sense of what is right and wrong, what is believable. But it is usually not enough to justify our beliefs. Even if our instincts are good, we normally need other explanations, other reasons and other information to make a belief worth holding. And our instincts can sometimes, with this other information, prove to be misguided.

I BELIEVE BECAUSE ... IT MAKES LOGICAL SENSE

A further explanation for why we hold certain beliefs is that they make sense when we reason them through. This differs from intuition, which is often just an impression or a sense that something is true. Here, we believe it to be true because it makes logical sense.

This kind of belief often comes about through persuasive means. An intelligent speaker may present an argument for something, and you find yourself believing her. A sports coach explains to his team why he is confident that they can win the game, and they take on board his confidence as their own. The argument may be more or less formal, more or less tight and carefully reasoned.

In *The Da Vinci Code*, such argument is sometimes used to persuade a character (and the readers) of a particular point. One important example is the discussion of the role of Constantine in the formation of the Bible and the shaping of the teaching that Jesus was divine.

Leigh Teabing's argument in the novel runs something like this:

1. Human beings aren't divine;
2. Christians believe Jesus was both human and divine;
3. Therefore, at some point in history, someone 'fudged' the idea that Jesus was divine.

It's hardly a tight logical construction, but it will do to get across the novel's account. As we know, Teabing proposes that Constantine declared Jesus to be divine in order to co-opt Christianity, the rising religion, to the empire of Rome:

> "By officially endorsing Jesus as the Son of God, Constantine turned Jesus into a deity who existed beyond the scope of the human world, an entity whose power was unchallengeable. This not only precluded further pagan challenges to Christianity, but now the followers of Christ were able to redeem themselves *only* via the established sacred channel—the Roman Catholic Church." (*The Da Vinci Code*, pp. 315-6/233)

The argument makes some sense, and is therefore quite believable. Constantine wanted to gather Christians into his endeavour rather than have them as opponents. He himself had some kind of conversion experience just prior to a famous battle (the Battle of Milvian Bridge in 312 A.D.) and had a vested interest in Christianity. He saw that elevating Jesus to divine status would give Christianity a high place in his pluralistic empire and keep Christians under the thumb of the new Church. In order to sustain this view that Jesus was divine, he got rid of any teaching or documentation that suggested otherwise. He also convinced a council of church figures (the Council of Nicea in 325 A.D.) to declare formally that Jesus was divine and to rubber-stamp the version of the Bible that he wanted to see in circulation.

It's a believable argument—until you start to look at the details, at which point it completely collapses. While the broad idea that Constantine might use political manoeuvring to keep Christianity where he wanted it has merit, the actual details of the events Leigh Teabing outlines do not match up with any of our knowledge of Constantine from history. There are so many mistakes in this section of the novel, that it is best simply to list them. If you want to pursue these details further, see the reading list at the back of this book.

- Constantine did not unify Rome under the single religion of Christianity in 325 A.D. (*The Da Vinci Code*, p. 315/232). It did not become the official religion until the reign of Emperor Theodosius at the end of the fourth century.
- There were not "more than eighty gospels" (*The Da Vinci Code*, p. 313/231) that taught the original history of Jesus as a mere mortal, so Constantine couldn't have destroyed them.
- By time of the Council of Nicea in 325,

Christians were already in broad agreement about which books were genuine and ought to be read as holy Scripture in the churches. There was never really any doubt that the books called Matthew, Mark, Luke and John, contained the true account of Jesus.

- Constantine did not collate, commission and finance a new Bible (*The Da Vinci Code*, p. 317/234). He did commission the distribution of Scriptures that were already authenticated by the Church.[4]
- The Council of Nicea did not vote on whether or not Jesus was divine. Jesus was already worshipped as more than a human from the early years after his death and resurrection. The Council did discuss the views of a priest called Arius, who was arguing that Jesus wasn't fully God, just a bit like God. The Council decided that Arius was wrong—in a landslide of 298 to 2.

The problem with beliefs based on argument is that they rarely can account for all the facts. They usually have to ignore some details, or try to squeeze them uncomfortably into the framework of the argument. Once again, evidence is required to justify holding a belief. Leigh Teabing's argument that Constantine is responsible for what we call Christianity today has its attractions. It makes political sense. But it makes a mockery of Leigh Teabing's claim to being a great historian. When it comes to the facts behind the argument, it just doesn't compute.

I BELIEVE BECAUSE ... I'VE EXPERIENCED IT

One powerful explanation for why we hold beliefs is that they have been shown to be true through our experience. That is, things have happened in our lives or we have observed things or perceived them through our senses, and we have interpreted that experience to form beliefs.

There is little point arguing with a person's experience. If someone tells you they saw a UFO, you are in no position to say to them "No, you didn't". Experience belongs to the experiencer, and can't simply be denied. But it can be challenged in other ways.

For example, you might ask the UFO spotter whether they had been taking any drugs on the night of their experience. That would provide an alternative explanation: it wasn't a real experience, but a mental one induced by medication.

Another approach is to question the *interpretation* of the experience: "How do you know it was a UFO? Could it have been your brother's new radio-controlled plane?"

A third approach is to suggest that the person is lying; you take this approach at great risk, but sometimes it might be a fair question.

Experience needs to be considered carefully, because it can be a good teacher and a good basis for beliefs. But it can equally be confusing and lead to wrong conclusions because of the impact it has on us.

The story of *The Da Vinci Code* is built on two elements of the experience of Christianity that many people report. The first is the experience of the Church as an oppressor. We have already discussed this in some detail. It is the second element that I wish to dwell on now—the experiences of women in the Church.

The Da Vinci Code suggests that women experience the traditional Church as a cold, masculine and oppressive institution. Most significantly, it suggests that a truer, more satisfying form of spirituality can be found by embracing the feminine and recovering what Robert Langdon calls the "sacred feminine". The novel argues that the foundations of ancient religion were in fertility, and that fertility belongs foremost to the female, not the male:

> "[T]his concept of woman as life-bringer was the foundation of ancient religion. Childbirth was mystical and powerful. Sadly, Christian philosophy decided to embezzle the female's creative power by ignoring biological truth and making *man* the Creator. Genesis tells us that Eve was created from Adam's rib. Woman became an offshoot of man. And a sinful one at that. Genesis was the beginning of the end for the goddess." (*The Da Vinci Code*, p. 322/238)

By re-experiencing the power of the feminine, we can recover a sense of true spirituality, Langdon argues. The feminine dimension is experienced in greater appreciation of nature, in the celebration of children, motherhood and family, and in a new attitude towards sex.

The renewal of sexuality is a theme that continually re-

emerges in the novel. It is an important plot element—
Sophie Neveu saw her grandfather engaged in a sex ritual
which disturbed her and she kept secret for 10 years. The
ritual was a kind of group sex act called Hieros Gamos
('sacred union', according to the novel). While Sophie was
very distraught as a teenager who witnessed this, Langdon
wants to reinterpret her experience in spiritual terms:

> "Historically, intercourse was the act through which male
> and female experienced God. The ancients believed that
> the male was spiritually incomplete until he had carnal
> knowledge of the sacred feminine. Physical union with
> the female remained the sole means through which man
> could become spiritually complete and ultimately
> achieve *gnosis*—knowledge of the divine [...] By
> communing with woman," Langdon said, "man could
> achieve a climactic instant when his mind went totally
> blank and he could see God". (*The Da Vinci Code*,
> p. 410/308-9)

The novel suggests that the experience of sexual intercourse will be a divine revelation—at least for the man!
Through the experience, he will come to know God.
Langdon tells Sophie that this spiritual empowerment was
a threat to the official church, and so they have for
centuries "worked hard to demonize sex and recast it as a
disgusting and sinful act" (*The Da Vinci Code*, p. 411/309). It
is hard to think of any examples of Christian churches that
explicitly or even implicitly do this. But for the sake of Dan
Brown's argument, a stark contrast is drawn between the

liberating experience of the divine through sex, and the oppressive anti-sensuality of organized religion.

But how well do these descriptions match with actual human experiences of either?

The reality is that every person's story is different. For some, sex is a liberating and vibrant part of their lives; for others, it is traumatic or disappointing. For some, church is experienced as anti-feminine, anti-sensuality and anti-nature. But for others, church has none of these negative elements.

This illustrates one problem with using experience as a basis for beliefs—experience is so varied between people. There is little stability in experience, such that reliable beliefs can be formed from it. Perhaps on one particularly special occasion for some individuals who have sex, the earth moves with ecstasy and they feel they make contact with the Beyond. But it would be astonishing if sexual experience provided this "moment of clarity during which God could be glimpsed" (*The Da Vinci Code*, p. 410/309) for human beings in any *dependable* fashion. Not all sex is good sex, let alone mind-blowing, mind-expanding, transcendent experience of the other. It may be that at this point, there is an element of wishful thinking going on.

Experiences are powerful and convicting. We take them seriously when we are forming our beliefs. But they can be unreliable, and need to be supplemented by other supports for belief.

I BELIEVE BECAUSE ... THERE'S EVIDENCE FOR IT

At many points throughout this book, we have made mention of 'the evidence' and that this evidence would be discussed later. We have reached that point. Having considered a number of the explanations for why we hold our beliefs, we come to one of the strongest—because there is evidence for the belief.

Evidence is anything that is explained by the belief and supports the belief—objects, writing, people, facts. These can all constitute evidence for a belief. We most often talk about evidence in legal situations, but we can talk about the evidence for any kind of belief.

Speaking personally for a moment, I'm always looking for evidence that my wife loves me (call me paranoid). Fortunately, there is plenty of evidence to be found: she says she loves me, she tells other people that she loves me, she shows concern for what I am doing, she wants to spend time with me, she stood up in front of a large group of people many years ago and said, "I will". All of these actions and words constitute evidence for my belief that Amelia loves me.

Some things are said to be 'self-evident', by which it is meant that, if your brain and your senses are working properly, you will just recognize that some things are true. All humans everywhere ought to be able to assent to those beliefs. An example of this is the United States Declaration of Independence:

We hold these Truths to be self-evident, that all Men are created equal, that they are endowed by their Creator with certain unalienable Rights, that among these are Life, Liberty and the pursuit of Happiness.

It would be interesting to know how many Americans agree today that all of these beliefs are self-evident. We are, in our postmodern age, rather sceptical about claims that truth is self-evident.

In this book, we have tried to explore the reasons behind why *The Da Vinci Code* has been so popular, and whether the views that it expresses about Christianity are worth believing. We've acknowledged the possible reasons why people are actually believing the claims of the novel, as well as exploring why it is that we believe anything. We've tried to understand why people are adopting the views the novel presents, but the biggest objection to these views arises with the question of evidence.

The beliefs that the characters in the novel espouse, especially Leigh Teabing and Robert Langdon, are simply not well supported by evidence.

Indeed, some of the views they espouse are either seriously questioned or entirely discredited by the evidence.

Let's take two major views, ones that are significant to the Christian faith.

First, consider the claim that there were thousands of documents recording that Jesus was a mortal man, and that these were destroyed under Constantine (*The Da Vinci Code*, p. 317/234). What is this referring to? The documents on view are known as *The Nag Hammadi Library*, named after the place in Egypt where they were discovered in 1945, as we mentioned earlier. They are sometimes called 'the Gnostic Gospels', but this is something of a misnomer, since 'gospels' is the wrong genre classification for most of them.

There aren't thousands of them, as Teabing pontificates, but there are 45 ancient fragments that appear to have come from a library, since they are bound into 12 codices (or books) plus some smaller tracts. They were translated into English in 1977 and some of them can be found on the web.[5]

Leigh Teabing makes remarkable claims for these documents:

> "The scrolls highlight glaring historical discrepancies and fabrications, clearly confirming that the modern Bible was compiled and edited by men who possessed a political agenda [...]" (*The Da Vinci Code*, p. 317/234)

But what does the evidence itself suggest? Does it support or dismantle such views?

The first question concerning these documents is their date of composition. It is agreed by almost all scholars that most of the 45 documents were written in either the mid-second or third centuries A.D. That is, they were written at least 100 years after Jesus. Compare this with the composition dates accepted by most scholars for the New Testament books: most think the New Testament was largely complete by 100 A.D.

This means that any evidence we glean from *The Nag Hammadi Library* is pre-dated by the information in the Bible. In other words, the Bible has the most ancient (and therefore most likely to be true) information. If any discrepancies are being revealed, they are going to be in the later documents.

The second question to ask is: what kind of documents are these?

When you read them, you find that they are not very much like the Bible at all, especially when it comes to information about Jesus. In the Bible's Gospels, we have three strongly historical narratives of Jesus birth, early life, teachings and miracles, and then his path to crucifixion and then resurrection (see Matthew, Mark and Luke). In the Gospel of John, we have a more stylised and poetic account of Jesus' teachings, miracles and passion events. But even the *Nag Hammadi* texts with the word 'Gospel' in the title (e.g. *The Gospel of Truth*, *The Gospel of Philip*, *The Gospel of Mary*) are very different from the "orderly account" (Luke 1:3) that Luke set out to write. Only *The Gospel of Thomas* looks anything like a biography of Jesus. For example, *The Gospel of Philip* is a series of statements about light and darkness, baptism, marriage, adultery and overcoming evil. It contains some mention of Jesus (and Mary Magdalene, as we shall see), but it is not a narrative of Jesus' life. In comparison with the biblical texts, the Gnostic texts are extremely obscure, fragmented, and difficult to make sense of. These various fragments and so-called gospels are easily available to interested enquirers, so that they can make their own comparisons with the Bible's accounts.

Third, what is made in the Gnostic texts of Jesus' divinity? Bizarrely, the novel claims that these ancient texts championed Jesus' humanity. In fact, the opposite is true— they denigrate humanity and the flesh; in fact, they find sex repulsive in a way which clashes directly with reports in the *The Da Vinci Code*.

Far from providing evidence for the inaccuracy of the Bible, the *Nag Hammadi* texts highlight how very historically reliable and unusually coherent the biblical texts are. There is no other ancient documentation like them.

Second, let us consider the evidence for Jesus being married to Mary Magdalene. We might briefly ask just how important the outcome of our enquiry is to Christian belief. Does it matter whether Jesus was married? Could he have been the Son of God and yet be married and a father? Is there any theological problem with that?

A few points can be made. Christians believe that Jesus was fully and properly human. Without getting into detailed discussions about his DNA, we know that Jesus ate and drank, slept, had emotions, and even died, just like all other human beings. If marriage is simply part of human existence, then it is compatible with our understanding of Jesus. But to say anything beyond that would be speculation. For Christians also believe that "in him all the fullness of God was pleased to dwell" (Colossians 1:19), and so we cannot comment on how a divine being could marry. It's best not to try.

However, it can be said that having sex with his wife would not have been a defiling act, as the novel seems to suggest. In God's creation, sex in marriage is a gift to be treasured, and it certainly wouldn't have impinged on Jesus' divinity. Sex, properly practised, is a good thing in Christianity, not a sin.

Where, then, does Dan Brown gather this idea that Jesus and Mary Magdalene were married? It comes from his appropriation (and misquoting) of some passages from the Gnostic Gospels. Here are the two passages of interest:

Peter answered and spoke concerning these same things. He questioned them about the Savior: Did He really speak privately with a woman and not openly to us? Are we to turn about and all listen to her? Did He prefer her to us?

Then Mary wept and said to Peter, My brother Peter, what do you think? Do you think that I have thought this up myself in my heart, or that I am lying about the Savior? Levi answered and said to Peter, Peter you have always been hot tempered. Now I see you contending against the woman like the adversaries. But if the Savior made her worthy, who are you indeed to reject her? Surely the Savior knows her very well. That is why He loved her more than us. (*The Gospel of Mary*, 9:3-9)[6]

And the companion of the ... Mary Magdalene ... her more than the disciples ... kiss her ... on her ... The rest of ... They said to him, "Why do you love her more than all of us?" The saviour answered and said to them, "Why do I not love you like her? ..." (*The Gospel of Philip*, 63:31-64:11)[7]

These passages provide interesting stories of how the male disciples viewed Mary Magdalene, and how Jesus treated her. But are they evidence that the two were married? I think they fall well short. The word 'wife' or 'spouse' is never used—'companion' means a friend, and if Mary had been Jesus' wife then the obvious word would have been used. There was nothing to hide. Furthermore, in the novel (*The Da Vinci Code*, p. 331/246), Dan Brown fills in the gaps in the historical record. In the quote above from *The Gospel of Philip*, there are a few missing parts indicated by the ellipses. These indicate sections where we simply *do not know* what the words are. They have either been smudged, or the document is ripped, or there is a word missing due to scribal error. We don't know what should be there. But Dan Brown does—he tells us that Jesus would "kiss her often on her mouth". This interpolation raises the stakes for claiming this is evidence that they were married. Or does it? Even this sleight of hand from the author does not convince historians that it is a claim to marriage. If that happens to be the original text, it is most likely to be the common kiss of brotherly Christian greeting that is on view for the author (see, for example, 1 Peter 5:14).

As fascinating as these ancient fragments are, they are hardly sufficient evidence to support the view that Jesus and Mary were married. If you have this belief, or are considering adopting it, you must be doing so on the basis of 'the vibe' or 'logical sense', because the evidence just isn't there.

Is there any reason why we should treat the Gnostic documents as anything more than fiction themselves? Their value for understanding Mary Magdalene is made crystal clear by the very editor of *The Nag Hammadi Library*, Professor James Robinson:

> I think the only relevant text for historical information about Mary Magdalene is the New Testament, and it does not go beyond saying that she was one of the circle of women who accompanied the wandering Jesus and his male followers.[8]

One of the strangest aspects of Dan Brown's novel is that it never quotes the New Testament. He never uses the most ancient sources we have for understanding who Jesus was. The sources Dan Brown uses to construct the novel's version of Christianity are not just unusual. They are, in fact, the *least reliable* historical records we have for understanding Jesus and the Christianity of the first few centuries after his death.

I BELIEVE BECAUSE ... SOMEONE I TRUST TOLD ME IT WAS TRUE

The final measure that we use to assess whether a belief is worth holding takes us back to the question of authority. From childhood, we trust certain people to tell us the truth, to educate us about the world, and not to lead us astray, since we are incapable of making our way on our own. This dependence carries on in life, often bludgeoned and sometimes totally destroyed by bad experiences with people who shouldn't be trusted.

Since we hold views because they are given to us by people we trust, if we are to reassess our views we will also have to reassess the trustworthiness of the people who gave them to us. Mark Twain reported the growing trust of a son in his father:

> When I was a boy of fourteen, my father was so ignorant I could hardly stand to have the old man around. But when I got to be twenty-one, I was astonished at how much the old man had learned in seven years.[9]

Trust can grow or diminish over time, affecting the beliefs from which it was generated. I know mentors who have undone the beliefs they instilled in their charges because they haven't lived up to their own claims.

Trustworthiness is a powerful affirmative tool for belief; and trust-breaching is equally destructive of the beliefs for which the trust was responsible.

So who can be trusted?

4 | I BELIEVE BECAUSE …

The answer from the culture of suspicion is 'no-one', but this is a little unfair. Perhaps 'no-one entirely' is fairer.

The account of religion in *the Da Vinci Code* depends on us trusting a certain character—Leigh Teabing. He is the source of most of the innovative ideas about the history of Christianity, the deceptions of Emperor Constantine, and the true nature of the Holy Grail.

This leaves us with a problem. Teabing, it turns out, is the ultimate bad guy—the Teacher. The one whom we need to trust in order to justify our belief in his claims about Christianity, has in fact shown himself to be a deceiver and a murderer. How can we trust him? Poor Silas, the tragic albino monk, is the symbol of misplaced trust. His passion for his Church and his love for his Bishop, Aringarosa, drive him to commit unspeakable crimes. But his loyalty was not rewarded; he was but a pathetic pawn in the game others were playing.

The Teabing affair brings the whole question of why we believe things into relief.

Here is someone who claims to offer the truth, to blow away the cobwebs of deception, and to liberate souls with his unveiling of true spirituality in the Mary Magdalene story. Anyone who offers such major prizes ought to be able to deliver them.

In contrast, this is where Christian belief seems to me to be very strong.

Christians believe that God revealed himself to the world in the person of Jesus, and that by what Jesus said and did—ultimately by dying for the sins of the world and rising victorious to new life—he made God known to all, and a relationship with him available to all.

Christians have confidence in this belief because of the trustworthiness of God. Throughout the Bible, a constant refrain is that God will never abandon his people—he may judge them, he may be angry with them, but he will not abandon them. Furthermore, the Bible emphasizes time and again that God keeps his promises. The Bible is full of such statements; here is a selection:

> Blessed be the LORD who has given rest to his people Israel, according to all that he promised. Not one word has failed of all his good promise, which he spoke by Moses his servant. (1 Kings 8:56)

> Righteousness and justice are the foundation of your throne; steadfast love and faithfulness go before you. (Psalm 89:14)

> Your kingdom is an everlasting kingdom, and your dominion endures throughout all generations. (Psalm 145:13)

> Let us hold fast the confession of our hope without wavering, for he who promised is faithful. (Hebrews 10:23)

This great emphasis on faithfulness is one of the huge encouragements of Christian faith. If it is not true, it is a major betrayal, because the trustworthiness and faithfulness of God are among its key teachings. Christians believe that Jesus reveals God to us, and that we know Jesus through the

Scriptures. This is a belief many people grew up with, for whom it sounds right, makes sense, matches their experience and for which there is a good deal of interesting evidence. But ultimately, they come to believe because they trust the God that the message reveals to them.

CONCLUSION: BELIEVERS ANONYMOUS

Beliefs, then, can be held for many reasons. Sometimes these reasons are good; sometimes they are insufficient. Beliefs can be changed, even if we are not totally in control of them, and they must be scrutinized regularly. *The Da Vinci Code* has provided many people with that 'house fire' experience where they have had to begin again and consider what is worth believing.

In this book, I have tried to explain what in *The Da Vinci Code* seems worthy of belief, and what comes up short. Judging by the enthusiastic reaction many people have had to the novel, I sense we may need to value our beliefs more highly than we do. We need to be more protective of them and more discerning.

What steps can an avid *Da Vinci Code* devotee take to ensure he or she is only believing things that are worth believing? We need something a bit like AA—Believers Anonymous. It could develop into a twelve-step program, but for now there are five steps that recovering *Da Vinci Code* believers can take:

1. Admit that we have a problem and acknowledge we are not totally in control of it. We have been attracted to various beliefs on offer in the novel that might seem true to us or match with some aspects of our religious experiences, but for which there isn't good evidence.

2. Have a good look at ourselves to work out why we were attracted to the views (was it family, personality, teachers, experiences with religion, etc?).

3. Work step-by-step to examine these beliefs. This book has been a start. There are further reading suggestions up the back of the book. I highly recommend a return to the most ancient documents on Christianity, found in the pages of the Bible itself. Having explored some ideas with me in this book, you may see the Bible a little differently than when you last read it.

4. Express your anger, then accept an apology. If you are angry with the Church in the manner this book discussed, then you may need to express that anger to someone. But having done that, I hope that you will accept the apologies offered for the way the Church has on occasion scandalously hidden secrets within its ranks, for the way women are perceived and treated in some parts of the Church, and for the way traditional Christianity just hasn't captured the imaginations of many people today. Given that Christians find the story of Jesus so exciting and so life-changing, it really shouldn't come across as boring and conservative.

5. Pray. If there is a God, he will hear your prayer and answer it. You can do this while reading, while thinking—at any time. A prayer offered up quietly can be the beginning of a new sense of trust, and the beginning of the end of the Teabing affair.

ENDNOTES

1 C. S. Lewis, *Surprised by Joy*, Geoffrey Bles, London, 1955, p. 223.

2 Eric Mader-Lin, *Priory of Sion added to terrorist list*, Eric Mader-Lin, 19 May 2005, viewed 23 August 2005, <http://www.necessary prose.com/prioryonlist.htm>.

3 Denise Budd, 'Trying to make sense of Leonardo's "Faded Smudge"', in Dan Burstein (ed.), *Secrets of the Code: The unauthorised guide to the mysteries behind The Da Vinci Code*, CDS Books, New York, 2004, p. 229.

4 Eusebius Pamphilus of Caesarea, *The Life of the Blessed Emperor Constantine*, trans. Bagster, Book IV, chs. XXXIV-XXXVII, Internet Medieval Sourcebook, 1997, viewed 23 August 2005, <http://www.fordham.edu/halsall/basis/vita-constantine.html>. See discussion in Ben Witherington III, *The Gospel Code*, IVP, Downers Grove, 2004, pp. 63-5.

5 James M. Robinson, *The Nag Hammadi Library in English*, rev. ed., HarperSanFrancisco, San Francisco, 1990.

6 Robinson, *The Nag Hammadi Library*, p. 256.

7 Robinson, *The Nag Hammadi Library*, p. 148.

8 James M. Robinson, 'What the Nag Hammadi texts have to tell us about "liberated" Christianity', in Dan Burstein (ed.), *Secrets of the Code: The unauthorised guide to the mysteries behind The Da Vinci Code*, CDS Books, New York, 2004, p. 99.

9 Appropriately, although this quote is attributed to Twain in *Readers Digest*, September 1937, the source has not been identified so we cannot trust that it is in fact from Twain!

5 | MARY'S STORY

A story composed and expanded from the eleven biblical references to Mary Magdalene.

WHAT ARE THEY DOING TO ME? Oh, the shame. Why do they treat me like the Saviour, the risen One, the One to whom and in whom we will all rise, his people?

I met him when I was despairing of life. My body was in torment, my mind a rage. Demonic forces had hold of me and I longed to die. I was a sinner, a woman wracked by sickness and sorrow, and he offered me his love—he healed me in body and soul.[1]

He had power and authority; he spoke and even spirits responded. But why do they elevate me to places only the Lord can ascend? I am low and fallen, but he has lifted me up, like all of his people.

We walked with him and fed and tended him, women who owed him everything and saw in him the future that he proclaimed.[2] He preached about the kingdom, and we waited for the king.

You know what he said to us, of how he prayed for us, and there is no need to tell you. He has taught you and prayed for you, too. He was close to us, but close to you, too. Of course we loved him; we each wanted him; but he wanted all.

From this closeness, he moved away from us. He had to, to fulfil his mission.

And then, at the last, he was at a distance. And we, the women, were looking on.[3]

They cursed him at his death, on a cross, for nothing. And we were looking on. And we saw. And we remember what was done. And when he was dead, the one we all loved, we saw him laid in the tomb. We sat, and we saw his body buried, and the tomb sealed with a rolling stone.[4]

But, oh, the end was not the end. The tomb was not his final resting place. I still quake when I remember the dawn of the morning of the first day. The First Day.

I went to anoint the dead. The sun had just risen.[5] But I saw less than I expected. The stone was gone, and the Lord was gone. Death was gone—vanished!

I fled away in tears and fears,[6] but voices stopped me and asked me why I wept. How could they know? My Lord was taken.

Another voice persisted: Why the weeping, whom are

you seeking?

I turned to face the garden-tender, and he tenderly spoke to me alone, this time with a name:

Miriam, Mary of Magdala, my name.

The breath suddenly filled me, the heavenly breath of awakening, and then I breathed out, "Teacher!" and fell and clung on.

The teacher knew the clinging was for tomorrow, or tomorrow, or tomorrow, not today. The kingdom had come, but the king's homecoming was still to come.

I let go to run.[7] I went and told the heavy-hearted ones.[8]

And then they all came, and for a time we held hard onto his beautiful feet.[9]

And then we let go. And he went up.

He was not my spouse. He was *our* Spouse, our husband. We, his people, became his Bride. We belong to him and he gave all for us. And we will be together, forever, when the time has come.

He was not my spouse. He was my teacher, my lord and my God.[10]

ENDNOTES

1 Luke 8:1-3
2 Mark 15:40-41
3 Matthew 27:55-56; Mark 15:40
4 Matthew 27:61; Mark 15:47
5 Matthew 28:1; Mark 16:1

6 Mark 16:8
7 John 20:11-18
8 Luke 24:10
9 Matthew 28:9
10 John 20:16-18

FURTHER READING

On *The Da Vinci Code*'s claims regarding Christianity
Darrell L. Bock, *Breaking the Da Vinci Code: answering the questions everybody's asking*, Nelson Books, Nashville, 2004. A New Testament professor addresses the novel's claims about Christianity.

Ben Witherington III, *The Gospel Code: novel claims about Jesus, Mary Magdalene and Da Vinci*, Intervarsity Press, Downers Grove, 2004. Similar to Bock, but with more interaction with non-conservative New Testament scholars such as Marcus Borg and John Dominic Crossan. Ben Witherington III is professor of New Testament Interpretation at Asbury Theological Seminary in Wilmore, Kentucky.

On how we got the Bible
Paul Barnett, *Is the New Testament History?*, rev. edn, Aquila Press, Sydney, 2004. An introduction to the historical strengths of the New Testament.

Jeffrey L. Sheler, *Is the Bible True? How Modern Debates and Discoveries Affirm the Essence of the Scriptures*, HarperSanFrancisco, San Francisco, 1999. An investigative journalist traces the origins of the Bible.

Bruce Metzger, *The Canon of the New Testament: Its Origin, Development, and Significance*, Oxford University Press, Oxford, 1997. A detailed and scholarly account of the history of the New Testament documents.

On who Jesus is

The four Gospels in the Bible: Matthew, Mark, Luke, John. Why wouldn't they be top of the reading list?

The rest of the New Testament. The earliest record of Christian life and teaching.

John Dickson, *Simply Christianity*, Matthias Media, Sydney, 1999. An easy-to-follow journey into the biography of Jesus. Can also be done as a five-week course exploring the Gospel of Luke.

Paul Barnett, *The Truth about Jesus: the challenge of evidence*, Aquila Press, Sydney, 2004. An examination of what we know about Jesus from history.

P. Copan (ed.), *Will the Real Jesus Please Stand Up? A debate between William Lane Craig and John Dominic Crossan*, Baker Books, Grand Rapids, 1998. For those who want to read scholarship on all sides of the question.

On Gnosticism and the sacred feminine

Both Bock and Witherington above have good chapters on this.

On the history of the early church

Gerard Bray, *Creeds, Council and Christ: did the early Christians misrepresent Jesus?*, Christian Focus Publications, Fearn, 1997. An exploration of the debates about Jesus' identity in the early centuries after Christ.

Henry Chadwick, *The Early Church*, Penguin, London, 1993. The standard introduction to the history.

On belief and knowledge

James W. Sire, *Why Should Anyone Believe Anything at All?*, IVP, Downers Grove, 1994.

William Lane Craig, *Reasonable Faith: Christian Truth and Apologetics*, Crossway, Wheaton, 1994. A rational defence of Christian beliefs.

Gregory E. Ganssle, *Thinking About God: First Steps in Philosophy*, IVP, Downers Grove, 2004. A careful guide to tackling big questions of belief.

Thomas V. Morris, *Making Sense of It All*, Eerdmans, Grand Rapids, 1992. An exploration of life's meaning using the Christian philosopher, Pascal.

 **matthiasmedia**

Matthias Media is an independent Christian publishing company based in Sydney, Australia. For more information about our resources, and to browse our online catalogue, visit our website:

www.matthiasmedia.com.au

How to buy our resources

1. At Christian retailers everywhere—see our website for details of suppliers around the world.

2. Direct over the internet:
   - in the US: www.matthiasmedia.com
   - in Australia and rest of the world: www.matthiasmedia.com.au

3. Direct by phone:
   - within Australia: 1800 814 360 (Sydney: 9663 1478)
   - international: + 61 2 9663 1478

4. Trade enquiries:
   - email us: sales@matthiasmedia.com.au

Also available
from
Matthias Media …

According to Luke

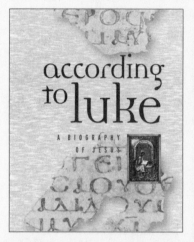

For an understanding of Christianity, it's hard to go past reading one of the Gospels for yourself. In the pages of these ancient documents, the reader meets the most powerful and compelling argument for the Christian faith: Jesus himself.

According to Luke is a fresh translation of Luke's Gospel by John Dickson and Tony Payne. Highly readable and beautifully produced, it also includes some short extra background articles about Luke's Gospel.

A Fresh Start

Probably the best-selling Australian Christian book of the last 20 years, John Chapman's clear, persuasive and engaging presentation of the good news of Jesus is as fresh and readable as ever. The book gives a straightforward explanation of our problem before God, his solution, how we can know it is all true, and what we should do about it. Highly recommended.

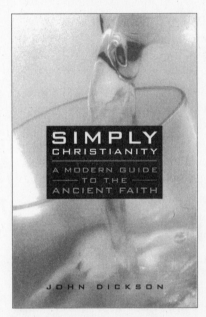

Two Ways to Live
CD-ROM

If you've ever wondered what Christians believe and why, but have never had the time or the inclination to read a whole book on the subject, then this CD-ROM is for you.

It features a simple and clear multi-media explanation of the core message of the Christian faith as found in the Bible—a message about God and his son Jesus, about life and death and the choice that we all face—as well as video answers to many of the most common questions about Christianity, such as:

- Did Jesus really come back from the dead?
- Is the Bible sexist?
- Hasn't science disproved Christianity?
- How do we account for all the suffering and evil in the world?
- What about other religions: are they all true?

Also included on the CD-ROM is a copy of a biography of Jesus' life (Luke's Gospel), and some personal testimonies of people who have become Christians.

If you're curious about Christianity, this resource is for you.

FOR MORE INFORMATION OR TO ORDER CONTACT:

Matthias Media

Telephone: +61 2 9663 1478 | Facsimile: +61 2 9663 3265
Email: sales@matthiasmedia.com.au

www.matthiasmedia.com.au

Jesus on Trial

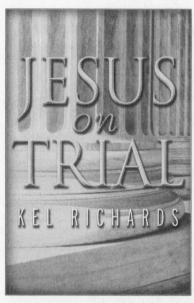

Popular author and radio commentator Kel Richards presents the evidence for Jesus' resurrection in a fresh and compelling way. Taking the analogy of a court case, *Jesus on Trial* demonstrates that the evidence for the resurrection satisfies our requirements of truth. The reader is in the position of juror, and is challenged to make a decision on the evidence as it is presented clearly and plainly by Kel. The appealing format and clear, simple writing makes this an easy book to give away to enquiring or sceptical friends.